The Future Home of The Woman's Institute

By the time this issue of INSPIRATION reaches you ground will have been broken for the erection of our new home. And by the end of the coming summer, we expect to occupy the beautiful structure pictured here-a monument erected in honor of all those who have made the Woman's Institute possible, a building amid pleasant surroundings in which we may continue to render the helpful service our constantly increasing student-body has every right to expect.

The image you see above was the illustration from the March, 1920 *Inspiration* newsletter that was published by the Woman's Institute of Domestic Arts and Sciences which inspired my book *Vintage Notions*. This was the correspondence school's fourth anniversary celebration issue. This building is still standing in Scranton, Pennsylvania and is now home to Scranton Prep High School. For a more modern look, I chose to update this edition with the cover artwork from the Spring 1926 issue of Woman's Institute *Fashion Service* magazine.

Edited by GUSTAVE L. WEINSS

Looking Ahead and *Building*

BY THE EDITOR

SOMEWHERE it is written, " 'Tis better to look ahead than to repine; 'tis better to build than to regret." This thought s e e m s particularly significant to me just at this time, for I have let you into what was a secret by showing to you as our cover design the future home of the Woman's Institute.

For several months, so many new students have been joining the Institute that we have been severely taxed to find sufficient space to accommodate our staff of workers. So this decision of the management to provide for us as quickly as possible a building in which we may expand is very welcome news.

WHILE this splendid new building seems like a reward for the service we have been rendering, we really feel that it will provide us a means whereby we can be of greater service to greater numbers, a place in which we can labor to better advantage for the good of our students. None can deny that we are progressing steadily, but that is what we hope to do right along—progress.

A recent letter contained this statement: "If my friends had told me a year ago that I would be the success I am today, I should have laughed at them; and, yet, all the while I had inside of me the feeling that I was progressing with my studies and preparing myself for just the success I am enjoying. Now that I am successful, I have the desire to do more, and I shall not be surprised if I awake some morning with my field of usefulness increased still more, for I intend always to be a student."

What this student has said expresses our ideas regarding our own achievements almost to the letter. And when we occupy our new home, we shall not be unmindful of the mission we have set out to perform—namely, to be of real assistance to all women by teaching them subjects that are of vital importance to them—and shall continue to improve ourselves for the better performance of our tasks.

BUT enough of this talk about ourselves. I should like to have you ponder over the thought that it is better to look ahead than to repine—better to build than to regret.

To look to the future with the spirit of hopefulness and then to plan and build so as to realize on your investment of time and labor is laudable indeed. The person who spends not his time in idleness will have no cause for repining and no vain regrets. It is when we have no thought for the future and care not how we build that we encounter difficulties of the kind that we cannot readily surmount. But when we have in us the assurance that comes from thinking ahead and planning aright, we can overcome almost any obstacle.

THE past, as well as the present, is replete with examples that emphasize the wisdom of looking ahead and then building accordingly.

Look to the founders of our country. Did they not fathom the future and then build for posterity?

Look to Lincoln and to Roosevelt. Did not these men have visions? And did they not meet with the success of the great?

Look to Edison. Is he not a student of the future? And does he not receive the reward that comes to those who serve?

Look about you—in or near your own home town. Don't you know some men and women who are typical examples of persons with enough foresight to see what confronts them and with enough courage to plan and build well for their future welfare?

YOU may say, "This kind of talk is all well and good, but it means hard work." Ah, that's the point! Building for the future does mean real hard work, and many times the end you seek may seem far distant. But even so you will be the gainer. No one ever loses by working for good. Discouragements may creep in; but it is true that happiness is a close ally of work, and if you were to get no greater reward than happiness, this would be enough.

But your reward will be greater, for just as a building is bound to be better when it is properly planned, so will your career be greater if you look ahead and plan for the future; and just as a structure will be more successful if the right kinds of materials are used in its construction, so will your career be more to your liking if you build with the materials that will permit you to progress.

In your endeavor to advance, then, be not misguided by the thought that you can get along well enough by taking life easy. Instead, be proud to work and bear in mind that " 'Tis better to look ahead than to repine; 'tis better to build than to regret."

Enthusiasm for Dressmaking

By MARY BROOKS PICKEN

Director of Instruction and Principal of
School of Dressmaking and Tailoring

WHEN I first realized that the real things of life are the things we feel and sense but never actually see with the eye, I was greatly concerned and the realization filled me with thoughts for many days. There is scarcely a time now when I am not conscious of the fact that life's biggest things we must sense but not see.

We feel Truth, yet we cannot describe it actually. We know that the spirit of God and man exists, yet we cannot see it with the naked eye. We know love to be real, but we are not conscious of the definite day or hour that it slipped into our hearts. We feel the kindness of our friends; we see their acts of thoughtfulness a l w a y s prompted by genuine kindness, but we cannot actually visualize kindness itself.

WHEN I was a youngster we had at home a white-china phrenologist's head, with all the different bumps outlined and named. My mother used this head very frequently to illustrate how our heads would develop. I know I experienced absolute fear at times lest my head should become bumpy in places that were not desirable, and I am sure that the constant searching for desirable bumps, such as Kindness, Truth, Love of Home, etc., stimulated their growth.

During the reign of this china head, I can remember having a very intense desire for a knowledge of sewing and dressmaking, colors and clothes, and I could not understand why this very wonderful china head did not contain a bump for dressmaking. As a child, I used to see pretty dresses and then wish very, very hard that I knew how to make them. I remember even now seeing featherbone catch-stitched beautifully in the seams of a basque and admiring the bones and stitches as though they represented something truly marvelous.

PEOPLE ask me when I learned to sew. I cannot say, because it seems that I always knew how to hold a needle and tie a knot, to gather evenly, and to hem skilfully. These things I learned when I was a very little girl. I never have been entirely conscious of receiving dressmaking knowledge at any definite time, but I have studied at every opportunity. I have always applied myself diligently, and it seems somehow my previous experiences have unconsciously fitted me for the new task.

I find in my Institute work that my own experiences are not singular. Each day I see students reaching out, doing more difficult and more creditable work, and to ask them when they actually became aware of their skill would be to get a negative answer, for I am sure they would not know. But of this I am sure—in talking with them you would find an open mind interested in knowing how and you would find hands that yearned to prove that they, too, could perform tasks of skill, for all of these go to produce knowledge of a subject and skill in execution.

I WAS in a very wonderful dressmaking workroom a short time ago. A woman was pointed out to me who had made linings for fifteen years, never anything else. The designer, whom I knew very well, told me that this woman was absolutely uninterested in any other part of dressmaking and was entirely unconscious of any other part of the work. She explained that she was sure this woman would not be able to make herself even a very simple dress. This was another proof of the virtue of an open mind, interest, and enthusiasm and of the value of learning by study and observation and never losing an opportunity for application.

The designer herself was a real inspiration, having started in three years before as an apprentice making linings under the direction of the fifteen-year lining woman. But this designer studied and applied every rule she could find, and her enthusiasm for smart clothes kept her ever on the alert. She constantly thought clothes and colors, she saw your costume instantly, and her keen eye evidenced her opinion, while her quick wit made you comfortable even if she didn't wholly approve.

AND this designer—may I write just a little more about her?—interested me greatly for several reasons. I was there with a friend who was having several gowns made. I watched carefully. The designer's mental preparation for each gown as it came to the fitting room was almost visible. She had just one brought in at a time, and as she chatted you could follow the trend of her thought. First she worked out a delightfully smart afternoon frock of navy silk, and all the while she was telling of a very smart tea one of her customers had attended. She was mentally there at that tea at that moment with her present customer, harmoniously fitting that particular frock into the setting. I need not tell you that it was an entire success. Every fold and bit of trimming was placed just as if this designer had a group of well-dressed women before her and was trying to have her customer outrival them all.

THE next to be brought in was a smart street dress to be worn with a scarf. Immediately the designer was talking of the Fifth Avenue church crowd of the previous Sunday and of some attractive street dresses she had seen, and then she confessed that only a few mornings before she had spent ten precious moments in front of a window where a very handsome street dress was displayed. I asked her to describe it to me. She hesitatingly answered, "Oh, it was so beautiful I cannot describe it, but I believe I can illustrate it." And I saw her fingers working at a soft fold at the waist which came around in sash effect and looped over a long, graceful panel at the back. Then I realized that she was interpreting anew the gown she had so thoroughly appreciated a few mornings before.

MY FRIEND remarked to the designer when she had finished the several fittings that she must be very tired. The designer answered: "Not tired, but mentally empty. I shall not do any more gowns today." As I saw the happiness in her face, I realized some of the joy a real artist experiences. It was a treat to see her work and to reflect her thoughts while she worked; then to see her satisfaction afterward was a stimulus much worth while. We sat down for a cup of tea and a little visit, and our talk drifted to certain women whom we all knew and who always appear well dressed.

Then the designer divulged some very sincere secrets. She told of the pleasure of creating clothes for women who wear them with enthusiasm, women who delight in b e c o m i n g clothes. Then she said, "I like to know a little of what's in a woman's heart before I make clothes for her. I like harmony in clothes as well as thought. The little nervous fidgety woman, you know, is inclined to choose very gay things and then feel very much frenzied w h e n she wears them. T h e l a r g e, c l u m s y woman is sure to select something drab and heavy looking, w h i c h i s bound to make her appear dull. Such things I try to avoid; yet I never audibly insist upon my way. Every woman knows by instinct when her dress is right for her individuality. When I succeed, we are both agreed and are both very happy."

Frocks for the *First Warm Days*

By ALWILDA FELLOWS
Department of Dressmaking

HAVE you ever stopped to consider the versatility required of the average home woman? Her life, by the casual observer, is considered rather monotonous. But let the casual observer step in and try to shoulder her responsibilities and assume even a part of her regular duties—a few days', perhaps even a few hours', experience will be the most convincing proof possible of her original misconception.

SUCH a variety of occasions for which the home woman must plan! The children's school clothes are no sooner finished and the children started off to school than canning must be completed and housecleaning begun. When housecleaning cares have been overcome because of the many days of effort put forth to make every nook and corner spick and span, Thanksgiving and Christmas needs must be anticipated and prepared for. Succeeding the holidays, the weeks with long, winter evenings afford opportunities to pick up odds and ends and, in a way, prepare for the busier days ahead. Then Easter preparations come with full force. This is the time when each member of the family must have apparel desires realized, for Easter without a new outfit, to youthful minds, is indeed colorless.

After Easter, attention must once more be directed to housecleaning and its incident redecorating or furnishing. Garden making must also be considered and hurriedly given a start, so that sewing for the summer, or more especially for last days of school, perhaps for graduation, may be accomplished.

Finally, the vacation rush with packing, more sewing, and an endless amount of preparation to be followed by a summer devoted perhaps to a few weeks of partial rest, but more probably to almost constant entertainment of guests, brings the average home woman to the beginning of another year. Just where has monotony had an opportunity to creep into her activities?

PREPAREDNESS is probably of more vital importance in homemaking than in any other profession. This is the keynote of the average woman's activities, for she knows that a smoothly running, well-ordered household is conducive to happiness and noble aspirations. Therefore, is preparedness not worth while?

Just a little in advance of the usual time for summer preparations is the suggestion that at least a part of the sewing may succeed the spring dressmaking and help, in a way, to lighten the work later on.

Shops have for some time offered a variety of light cotton fabrics. If selections are made while the stock is fresh and at its very best, they are bound to prove pleasing.

Each year seems to exceed the preceding year in the unusual features and real beauty of the fabrics that are produced. Cotton is no longer placed in the ordinary class in which we need to consider it; the summer season will undoubtedly usher in a popularity for cotton fabrics that has not been exceeded for some time.

PRINTED Georgettes and chiffons ranging from the quaintest of old-fashioned flower designs to the more daring color schemes of today display real beauty and have already proved their desirability by the way in which they are sought. These printed silk fabrics are shown in many of the spring frocks and, without doubt, their popularity will extend throughout the summer. But a variety of lovely patterns is being introduced in cotton fabrics, also, and printed cottons will be considered very smart for the summer season.

Inspiration for the designs in the printed cottons has been taken from various sources. Old English chintz patterns in attractive, indistinct color schemes are applied to voile, organdie, and occasionally to batiste. Small, old-fashioned calico patterns are applied to batiste, and especially to satine of fine, excellent quality. The revival of dotted Swiss is another characteristic note of the season. This is made entirely of one color, in white with colored dots, and in colors with white dots.

Organdie and voile in plain colors, net, and gingham make up the remainder of the most popular cotton fabrics. Linen, also, will be good, but prices are almost prohibitive in the better qualities of this fabric.

TO RETURN to printed Georgettes, the dresses made of this fabric are very lovely. Many of them have portions of the designs outlined in beads, and to carry out this trimming idea further, looped fringe of the beads is artistically used. Taffeta, as was predicted, has made a nation-wide appeal. It is probably the leader among spring fabrics, but as the season advances, high-luster silks and failles of very fine weave will be in great demand.

Blouses in soft kimono effect are particularly attractive when developed in printed Georgette. A style similar to the one shown at the upper left, if made of this material, might have frills of plain color and trimming of beads used to outline the designs in the front. This blouse would be very lovely, also, in a pastel shade of organdie with embroidery in silk or wool floss.

Tricolette in rather vivid colors is at present enjoying unlimited popularity for blouses. This material is so rich in appearance, especially in the bright colors, that it is generally cut on rather severe lines and relies on touches of hand embroidery for its only trimming. The style usually shown is similar to the one on this page, but the frills and sash are omitted. To learn the price of these blouses ready-made is to experience a sort of shock, but as they can be so easily and quickly made at home, the woman who sews may indulge in one or more of them for wear with her Easter suit.

THE first warm days follow soon after Easter. What an extreme satisfaction it is to be prepared for them with a new frock or two of the popular summer fabrics. Fashion is still maintaining its kindly attitude in regard to simplicity of construction as applied to cotton frocks. Many of the new styles retain the straight gathered skirt from which we have derived so much satisfaction. More than this, Fashion is giving special consideration to kimono sleeves.

An example of simple but effective trimming characteristic of the easily made dresses now popular is illustrated by the dress of printed voile shown on this page. The contrasting fabric is organdie and the scalloped finish is formed by hem-stitching, in scalloped outline, two thicknesses of the organdie and then cutting the hem-stitching to form a picoted edge. The sash of self-material is lined with organdie.

Bias self-material is used effectively for trimming the gingham dress. Organdie, plain gingham, or chambray may be used for the cuff and the neck finish. This style is suitable for home wear or, in summer, may be used for street wear.

Hats for *Immediate* Wear

By MARY MAHON
Department of Millinery

ON A recent trip to New York, I had the pleasure of seeing an unusually large number of new hat models for spring. With their various shapes made of brilliant fabrics and braids and with unique and luminous trimmings of every hue, the general effect of these news hats is dazzling. Due to the enormous importation of French models this season, styles are so varied and materials so costly that at first glimpse one gets the idea that there seems to be no provision made for those who wish to wear the quiet, more modest hat. After giving some consideration and study to the contour and color combinations in the multitude of models, however, one finds that there are some particular features that are sure to appeal to every one's taste and requirements if they are worked out properly.

BUYERS returning from abroad tell us that the French women favor the close-fitting turban. This type of hat is draped with the different new fabrics and is worn squarely down on the head. It is rather short in the back, however, and thus does not hide the neck. In the words of one of the buyers, "The head continues to be worn well into the hat, accurately carrying out the lines of the Egyptian head dress, which is the influence most felt at the present time."

But this is surely bound to give way to something different at the hands of the American designer. Not all women desire the high-priced materials, nor are they inclined toward the extreme styles in hats. So, while such materials as the new lisophane, hair cloth, and cellophane are used to a great extent, practically all the new models can be carried out effectively in domestic fabrics and braids at one-third the cost.

CREATORS of fashion never before indorsed the rolled-brim hats so much as they do at present, and this is chiefly due to the fact that this particular shape is becoming to so many different types, bringing as it does the eyes and the back of the neck—both attractive in most women—into prominence. Such a hat can be made entirely of braid combined with either cotton crêpe or Georgette crêpe, and it can be trimmed in various ways—with a wreath of flowers around the crown or with a band of ciré ostrich around the edge. Or, if the more severe, tailored effect is wanted, a pretty wreath design may be embroidered around the crown. If it is desired not to spend too much time on hand work, one of the many pretty flower motifs done in raffia may be adopted. The motif serves as a nucleus, or center, and may be appliquéd to the side crown with long and short stitches of single strands of raffia. Such designs make an astonishingly good substitute for genuine hand work. In addition, a suitable trimming can be provided by making little flowers out of small pieces of velvet and silk and embroidering them with raffia.

ONE enticing model made on the rolled-brim shape had an under brim, or facing, of navy-blue Georgette, while the top of the hat consisted of bright, shiny visca braid in middy blue. This new shade of brilliant blue has a rich, glowing tone that is arresting much attention. The trimming consisted of a wreath of flowers made of cellophane in the different shades of castor combined with green and soft tones of copper. A band of two-tone No. 5 ribbon, with a chic bow directly at the back on the edge of the brim, gave the desired youthful effect that is so much sought in hats.

THE next hat in favor is the one that turns back off the face. This type of hat, though worn very much during the past season, is still occupying a prominent place in millinery, and the indications are that it is sure to continue in popularity for some time. This particular shape has many possibilities for the milliner, as it can be trimmed in so many ways. A very striking model carried out on this shape was made of satin braid in the soft, restful tone of cinder. The entire outside of the brim was made of rose petals in a deep shade of pink, aptly called arbutus, which gives the right dash of color to a gray outfit. The most unusual thing about this hat was a narrow, picot-edged ribbon in shades of sulphur and blue, which intermingled with the rose petals and continued to the right side, where it was finished with a bunchy bow.

The principal virtue of the shape that turns back off the face is that a veil may be worn with it very satisfactorily. And since veils are much in vogue, it follows that the hat that produces the most graceful effect will share in popularity with the veil.

COLOR combinations seem to be the most important thing in the realm of fashion and the thing that makes an imperative demand. Particularly is this true in millinery. Color is a prime factor in this art, for with an unhappy color scheme, many a smart shape and otherwise becoming hat is entirely ruined. An intelligent study of color and its relation to her own individual type will enable nearly every woman to eliminate the use of contradictory colors, which, as we all know, tend to mar her general appearance. As a hat serves as a frame for the face, it is very important that proper consideration be given to the color used in the facing. Therefore, the aim should be to avoid any trying colors or contradictory shades when selecting material for such purposes.

Cheerful Notes

By VERA TUMAN
Department of Instruction

IN SPITE of old "High Cost" and his grim disregard for folks, they are coming all the time—these notes of cheer. From every part of the country and generally from women who have more than their share of difficulties, the little notes travel to the Woman's Institute, fairly singing with the spirit of the women who are winning.

There is a wonderful advantage in cultivating a cheerful attitude toward things. Work is made so much easier when there's a cheery bit of courage behind it. Difficulties help smooth themselves out when one attacks the problems with a cheerful feeling that "things are not so bad." Then, better service is always to be had from the butcher and the grocer for a cheery customer who realizes that mistakes and delays are bound to occur in business and who is ready to make allowance for these.

BUT if you have the idea that cheerfulness is a natural gift, well—it's no idea, but rather a false impression. A cheerful attitude may be acquired, and all that is needed to obtain it is the desire to make those around you happy. The time and the thought that a lot of women give to dusting bric-a-brac that has neither beauty nor purpose would be more than enough to make the start toward a more cheerful spirit in the home.

It is really a duty for all of us to lighten

the tasks of those with whom we come in contact by a cheery word or smile, but it seems to be the special privilege of women, because of their wonderful sympathy and their close union with all the members of the family, to be able to scatter the most cheer in this old world. Most of the members of the Woman's Institute seem to realize this, but if there are any who doubt the help of cheer—just try it out. You are bound to find that a magical bit of courage creeps in that will be well worth your effort. There is a scarcity of too many things just now and we are blaming one thing after another for conditions. But do you realize that you and I will be responsible if cheerfulness and smiles are scarce?

IF YOUR means provide enough for meat only three times a week, plan to make the other meals just as tasty and attractive as possible. Don't refer to the lack of anything. Sprinkle in a lot of cheer, and the folks will never know the difference.

If the material for little sister's frocks costs so much that trimming or the scrap of organdie for her frills must be reserved for just the "bestest" ones, why let her know it? Put in a cheery note by outlining a little bunnie's head on each corner of her collar and she'll be happy. Big sister's enjoyment of a school dance is often marred by the long discussion of "How can we afford an evening dress?" It isn't quite fair. Get together. Every one in the family wants her to go. You'll manage to have enough for the little silk required for her dress, and above all get the color she wants. A strip of silver ribbon, a tiny bunch of silk flowers, and a "love of a dress" results. There's cheer in that, and she'll be glad to wear, for the rest of the summer, ginghams that are a wee bit coarser than she really likes. There's always a desire to cooperate when there's cheer put into the thing.

SOME time ago a letter came from a little woman who told of a whirl of duties and difficulties on a farm. Under it all, though, there was a tone of cheer that was wonderful and worth passing on.

Mrs. Cheerful's husband had to go away a great distance on business, and on the day he left the best cow discovered an old paint can and licked off enough paint to become poisoned. No one knew what was wrong. After a five-mile drive for the veterinarian, he pronounced it pneumonia and did everything possible to save the cow, but she died. Then a second cow took sick and died, and it was not until the third one was sick that the paint was discovered in the barnyard. "We were mighty glad to save this third one," said Mrs. Cheerful in her letter. "Now that everything has been stored away safely for the winter and my canning is all done and I have the boys trained to handle the chores, I am going to do more sewing. I've tried to keep up with my lessons as well as I could during the past months, and now that I have more time I know I'll be able to accomplish more. I made my little girl a middy last week. Her big brother told her she looked as smart as any of the little girls in the city, and of course I was pleased. Oh, I have oceans of sewing and I am so eager to start it; but there's always something to claim attention on a farm and I may not be able to do as much as I like, for I enjoy my work here in this lovely big country, too. And, though I never lived on a farm until nine years ago, I am successful and must not slight anything."

Easter Novelties

By LAURA MacFARLANE
Editorial Department

WELL does Easter deserve its recognition as the most joyous holiday of the year. Christmas affords us an opportunity to bring good cheer to others by means of deserving gifts; Thanksgiving awakens in us a spirit of thankfulness for all the blessings that are ours; July Fourth arouses every particle of our patriotism. But Easter far exceeds each one of these days in both its significance and its possibilities.

The fact that Easter commemorates the Resurrection and marks the triumph of eternal life over death is sufficient reason to accord it the supreme place it occupies. But, when it comes, all nature lends her assistance. The long, hard winter is past. Spring is at hand. Everywhere flowers are budding and trees are bursting into life. Old Mother Earth is garbing herself anew in the gayest and brightest of colors. And so, if Nature can conquer death in this splendid manner, how much more significant becomes the great story back of Easter.

A NUMBER of very delightful customs are connected with the celebration of Easter and observed by old and young alike. The sending of colored eggs to one's friends as gifts is perhaps the most popular of these. This has come down to us through the ages from such early peoples as the Egyptians, Persians, and Romans, who regarded the egg as the emblem of the universe.

In more recent years, we have added the legend of the eggs being the gift of the Easter rabbit, so small bunnies have become as popular at this time as eggs and chickens. Surely every one of us grown-ups can recall how eagerly we scampered downstairs on Easter morning to see what the Easter rabbit had left for us. And now what pleasure we find in preparing little gifts for the young folks about us, for they should never be overlooked in this joyous, gladsome time.

DYEING or staining hard-cooked eggs is the general custom, but if one has a little time to devote to Easter preparations, gifts that will please the most fastidious child can be made with very slight effort. Instead of boiling the eggs, the contents may be removed and the empty shells then used as a foundation for all sorts of attractive little novelties. To empty the shell, make a small hole in each end, and then, with the shell held gently between the thumb and forefinger, put one end to the lips and blow through the hole until the contents have run out at the other end.

On the empty shells, which should preferably be pinkish yellow, paint little faces and complete the effect by adding cunning dresses and bonnets of crêpe or tissue paper in pretty colors. There is no end to the ideas that can be carried out in this way, some decorating the eggs to represent particular persons, such as figures in history, and others making animals or birds or something especially liked by the child for whom the gift is intended. Arms and legs can be added by means of wire, and feet and hands can be made with sealing wax.

No one need hesitate to undertake this work because of any inability to paint the faces or things that are to be represented. Very good results can be obtained by tracing the designs from books or picture cards and then transferring these to the egg shells. The outlines thus made may be touched up and any additional lines put in with the aid of a fine paint brush.

ANOTHER charming Easter gift can be made by using egg shells as receptacles for a few tiny flowers, such as crocuses. For these, make a rather good-sized hole in the small end of the egg and remove the contents through this opening. Then dye the shells, using purple dye for some and yellow for others. Put tiny yellow

crocuses in the purple shells, and purple crocuses in the yellow shells, taking care to select small bulbs and blossoms. The flowers will remain fresh for some time if the bulb is surrounded with a little moss or soil before being placed in the shell and then moistened frequently.

Miniature hanging baskets can also be made out of halves of egg shells dyed green by pasting a narrow ribbon over the edge to bind it and then attaching the end of a loop of ribbon to each side and covering it with a small bow. The basket thus made may be used for any tiny flower or fern and hung up by means of the loop.

CONFECTIONS also add much to the pleasure of old and young at Easter time. Any of the home-made varieties find favor, but bonbons, probably because of their dainty and attractive colors, seem to please the most.

A rather novel little box in which to send candies can be made at home in a very few minutes. Cut a circular piece of cardboard a trifle larger than you wish the box and a strip of the same material as long as the circumference of the circle and as wide as the height you desire the finished box to be. Paste the ends of this strip together, and to the band thus formed, attach the circular

piece of cardboard to form the bottom of the box, bending up the edge to make a good joining. Cover the box thus made with crêpe paper in any desired color and fill with candy. For the lid, cut another circular piece of cardboard a little larger than the box, and with a square of crêpe paper cover this by placing the cardboard in the paper and drawing the ends together on top at the center and tying them with narrow ribbon. A tiny bunnie or chicken nestles comfortably in the opening thus made. Can't you just imagine the joy and pride of the small boy or girl who is the recipient of such a box of candy?

Woman's Institute *Question-Box*

Long Gloves Again Popular

The fashionable, short sleeves are giving me much concern. Won't long gloves be favored so that one may, in warm weather, appear suitably dressed on the street even though a coat is not worn? Are gauntlet styles in gloves still good?
R. A. F.

Long gloves will most assuredly be worn to a very great extent. In kid, these gloves are almost prohibitive as to price, but the long silk glove is a sanctioned substitute. The arm portion in some styles of both kid and silk gloves is quite elaborately embroidered.

Gauntlet styles apparently have lost none of their popularity. A prominent color in the showing of these styles, as well as in the other styles of gloves, is beige in a very light shade. A feature of the spring gauntlets is the elaboration of the inside of the cuff portion. In some of the higher-priced models, a bracelet effect is formed by running metallic ribbon through slits made at the wrist. The ends of the ribbon are finished with tassels and are tied to hold the glove close to the wrist.

Buttons for Blouses and Dresses

What kind of buttons are used for trimming blouses and dresses?
E. E. C.

Self-covered buttons are very good, especially for silk frocks that are not of an extremely dressy type. Georgette blouses and frocks very often favor cut-glass buttons in bright colors. Fancy jet, metal, bone, and celluloid buttons are used for novelties.

Want to Get Acquainted?

The following Institute students desire to become acquainted with other Institute students residing in their localities:

Northern Utah	T. N. B.
Orange, Tex.	E. A. K.
Cresskill, N. J.	A. F. L.
Hilo, Hawaii	K. G.
Schenectady, N. Y.	G. M. F.
United States or Canada	F. S. B.
San Antonio, Tex.	A. R.
Pottstown, Pa.	J. B. F.
Los Angeles, Calif.	J. P. H.
Baltimore, Md.	F. C. H.

I should like to become acquainted with some other Institute student living in Bakersfield, who is taking the Millinery Course.
MRS. WINIFRED MAINHART,
1722 H St., Bakersfield, Calif.

I should like to become acquainted with another student residing in Wichita, Kans. who is studying the Cooking or Dressmaking Course. H. H.

I should like to correspond with some of the students taking the Dressmaking and Tailoring Course who are under 25 years of age. P. G.

I should like to correspond with students taking the Complete Dressmaking Course with the idea of teaching sewing. H. B.

I should like to meet another Millinery student in Point St. Charles, Montreal, Que., Can.
G. M. D.

I should like to know if there is a Woman's Institute student residing in Washington, D. C., studying the Complete Dressmaking Course, who would be likely to desire a position in a shop where she could get an all-round experience. I can find employment for one first-class student who desires to earn while she learns. M. F.

I should like to become acquainted with Dressmaking and Millinery students. H. M. G.

I wish to become acquainted with some Institute students residing in West Haven, Conn.
L. R. B.

If other Woman's Institute students would like to get in touch with the inquiring students, we shall be glad to supply the addresses.

Model Samplers

Would you please send me models for all the samplers required in the next lesson? Mine are not as perfect as I should like them to be.
H. W. H.

It would not be giving you the best help to provide models for you to work from. Do the work as well as you can and send the results to us for correction. In this way we can see just the kind of work you are capable of doing and will be better able to assist you. You should not expect perfect workmanship at the very start. By this plan you will gain as you study, and when you are advanced in the work you will thoroughly appreciate it.

Corrected Samplers

If there is a correction made on a sampler and you give a percentage, is it necessary for me to send a corrected sampler? W. E.

When a percentage is given on a lesson, no further work on that lesson is required.

Materials for Hats

So many calls have come for spring millinery supplies that our Merchandise Service Department has necessarily had to prepare for them. Certain millinery materials are mentioned in Miss Mahon's article. If you cannot procure these from your local dealer, tell us your wants, stating color, kind, price limit, etc., and we shall be pleased to serve you.

Fitting Sleeves

A blouse I made recently is satisfactory in every detail except the sleeves, which draw through the upper portion with even the slightest movement of my arms. How can I overcome this trouble? M. G. K.

It may be that you did not give the proper attention to the fitting of the waist. If this is supposed to have a normal arm-hole line, see that the shoulder seam does not extend over the tip of the shoulder. If you find that no change is necessary in the waist portion, observe the armhole curves of the sleeve in order to determine whether or not these curves have been properly placed. A sleeve that, when folded lengthwise through the center, shows a marked difference in the armhole curves should be placed in the armhole so that the sleeve seam is from 1 to 2 inches—or for large figures a trifle more—in front of the under-arm seam and the upward curve is at the front. Then the opposite, or downward, curve will naturally fall in its correct position at the under arm. A close study of Art. 50 of the lesson Tissue-Paper Patterns, Part 1, will help you in fitting a sleeve that does not seem correct even after the rules for inserting it have been followed.

If no very decided difference between the armhole curves is noted when the sleeve is folded lengthwise through the center, this is generally an indication that the sleeve and under-arm seams may be made continuous. In this case, the higher curve should be placed at the back.

Applying Crocheted Yoke

How should I apply a crocheted yoke to a night-gown in order to make the finish very neat and inconspicuous? V. E. R.

If the nightgown has no fulness to be gathered to the yoke, pin and baste the yoke in position; then, from the right side, secure the edge of the yoke with close overhanding stitches. When the entire yoke is secured, cut away the material underneath to within a seam's width of the yoke edge. Then turn a narrow hem toward the yoke and secure it with fine stitches or form a tiny rolled hem and overcast it.

If considerable fulness is to be gathered into the yoke, this can be most easily and satisfactorily taken care of by first cutting the neck edge of the nightgown to correspond with the yoke shape. To finish the upper edge of the nightgown, make a rolled gathered hem; then whip the gathered and yoke edges together.

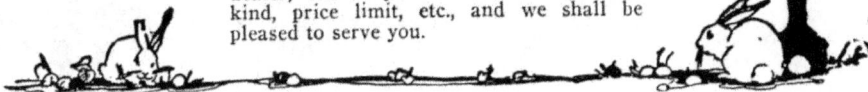

Our Students' Own Page

A $100 Dress for $28.50

In these days of the high cost of clothes, the woman who can make her own clothes has a decided advantage over her less fortunate sister who must pay the extremely high prices asked for ready-mades or make her old clothes do. This was illustrated in a letter received just a little while ago from one of our Clarksville, Iowa, members, Miss Lela R. Burroughs, in which she said:

I made a coat and a dress for myself and am real pleased with both. The material, buttons, etc., for the coat cost a little more than $50, but I priced the ready-made coats that were made almost like mine and they were more than $100. The material, trimming, and hem-stitching for the dress was $28.50 and the ready-made ones were selling for $100.

My dress is dark-red Georgette over dark-red satin. I stamped a design on the Georgette overskirt, ends of sleeves, and around the front of neck and worked it with beads and silk floss.

A Charming Evening Dress for $15.70

That sounds like a page out of "Alice in Wonderland" or some of the other fanciful fairy tales with which we were so charmed as children. But it isn't the subject of a fairy story, as the following letter from Mrs. Gladys Hunt, of Bury, Quebec, will indicate:

You helped me so with the ideas and illustrations on evening dresses that I thank you heartily. Now I am going to tell you about the little dress I made that called forth so many praises and compliments. I believe I mentioned to you before that I could not afford anything elaborate. My satin cost me $13.75, the tulle $1, net for the underslip 70 cents, belting 15 cents, straps 10 cents, making a total cost of $15.70. Very reasonable, was it not? I made the bodice of gold lace, and to soften it covered it with the tulle. The skirt of the dress was plain and narrow, with a draped overskirt. In making it this way, my satin is cut in such a way as to enable me to make it over again any time.

My friends paid prices ranging from $56 to $100 for their gowns, but I felt quite comfortable in my little $15.70 one, as well as having the satisfaction of knowing that I had accomplished something.

To Teach Her Daughters to Sew

Just how much the Woman's Institute is meaning to many of our members is reflected in the following letter from Mrs. Alberta Back, of Essington, Pennsylvania. The actual ability to make one's own clothes is really only a small part of the benefits derived from membership in the Institute. Mrs. Beck writes:

I want to say that I have put all I have learned so far into practice and I have never enjoyed sewing as I have this season. The little folks looked better than they ever did. Before, when I got a dress done, I could see I could have improved it in many ways. Now when I get the dress done, I am thoroughly satisfied with it.

I know with my amount of work it will take me a long time to finish my Course, but I will have learned so much that I will be content to work hard along with all I have to do, and I know you will have patience with me. In two years my oldest girl will take up sewing in school, and I am so glad she will have my textbooks to teach her the right way from the beginning. I am learning a pleasant way to sew, and my interest in everything is changed so much and I am so glad the change came within my reach to accomplish.

Making Her Self-Supporting

The following letter from one of our Pennsylvania members is a story in itself, and we are going to pass it along without comment, other than to say that for reasons that you will readily understand we are withholding the identity of the brave little woman who wrote it:

In October of 1918, I was suddenly confronted with the fact that I had to support three children, when my husband was taken from me during the influenza epidemic. I was at my wits' end as to how I would be able to keep my little family together. Then one day I read about the Woman's Institute of Domestic Arts and Sciences, in the *Modern Priscilla*. I spoke to my sister-in-law about it, and she said she had a booklet at home, called "Dressmaking Made Easy." I asked her whether I might see it, but sent for your booklet and literature at once. I had quite some knowledge of sewing already, as I did all the sewing for my family, but I did not have confidence enough in myself to start dressmaking. But I knew it was necessary to do something immediately, so I read and thought over the literature you had sent to me. I finally decided I would be able to take the Course in Professional Dressmaking, if I could pay for the Course on the instalment plan.

My wish was to do something that I could be in my own home and keep my children from the street, which is impossible if the mother works in a factory and puts the kiddies with strangers during her working hours.

I enrolled as a student during the early spring of 1919, and I am sure I cannot tell you how very interesting and helpful the lessons have been thus far. I thought I knew quite a lot about plain sewing, but soon realized how very little I did know, and how much harder and round about my methods were compared with your method.

I have all the work ahead that I can do for the next two months, which will surely prove to you more than words can, that your Course in Professional Dressmaking has helped me wonderfully.

I cannot thank you enough for the Institute, which is making it possible for a woman to be independent if she will but have enough interest in her future to get out of the rut and get down to work and never stop until her goal is reached.

Dressing Better at Half the Cost

The following letter from Mrs. Luella B. Clark, of Montpelier, Vermont, answers so clearly and frankly the question of the woman who doesn't know whether she can afford a Course that we are going to reprint it just as she wrote it:

I enjoy my lessons, every one more and more. I never thought that dressmaking would be so interesting as it is. There were some of my friends who thought it was foolish of me to spend time and money that way, but they were surprised when I showed them the books and explained the drafting to them. My sewing is improving all the time, and my husband often speaks of how nicely it is done. I think if more poor people like myself would take it up, they could dress much better and on half the money they now spend. I know I can. But it is hard to make some people understand anything like that. All they seem to look at is the price, and it never seems to occur to them that one's knowledge of dressmaking can be used long after the Course is paid for. To tell the truth, I didn't think, when I began, that I would get along as well as I have.

Where There's a Will, There's a Way

The following letter from Mrs. Annie K. Steere, of Littleton, New Hampshire, relates an experience that is probably typical of that of hundreds of our members. She didn't see how she was going to meet her payments. But it is strange how the way usually opens up when one resolutely attempts some worth-while accomplishment. Mrs. Steere wrote:

I had thought several times when I had read your advertisements that I would write, but was afraid to, for I thought that anything as good as that would be far beyond my means. But at last I decided that the only way to know would be to write, and the answer came telling about the monthly-payment plan. I did not know then how I could manage even that, but the more I thought about it the more I wanted the Course, and so I joined the Institute feeling sure that in some way I could earn the money. Since I joined, you would be astonished at the amount of work I have done. At Christmas time I did a lot of plain sewing, have made a dress for a friend, and am going to make two more soon. So it shows again that "Where there's a will, there's a way." I am not going to say that everything goes easy, for that would not be true, but since taking the Course I have grown very much more particular than I was. What would have suited me once does not suit me any more.

Fashion Service

SUPPLEMENT

Each Issue of *Vintage Notions Monthly* includes a *Fashion Service Supplement*. You will read about the fashion styles popular in the early twentieth century and receive a collectible fashion illustration to print and frame.

The students of the Woman's Institute would also receive a publication called *Fashion Service*. Where the *Inspiration* newsletter instructed them on all aspects of the domestic arts, not only sewing but also cooking, housekeeping, decorating, etc., *Fashion Service* was devoted entirely to giving current fashions with a key to their development.

Fashion Service prided itself on providing it's readers with reliable style information and the newest fashion forecasting. The publication wasn't just eye candy. The Institute stressed the importance of studying the fashions to benefit the sewer's understanding of dressmaking. To quote founder Mary Brooks Picken, "Once the principles of design...and of construction… are understood, beautiful garments will result. This publication comes to you as an aid to this desired goal. Read the text of every page and reason out the why of every illustration and description that your comprehension of designing and construction may be enlarged and your appreciation made more acute."

Today, these articles and illustrations give us a historically accurate view of what fashion really meant 100 years ago. Not only can we study these articles for an "of-the-time" style snapshot, but just as their students did, we can also learn to understand the principles of design and increase our sewing skills. In each issue, look for a collectible illustration in the back of the supplement!

Straight-Line Dress

To see the fashions of today with the varied positions of the waist line evidencing Victorian tendencies, which include the Empire, the Directoire, and the Basque, one trembles a wee bit, as when stepping on a foot-bridge at night and not being entirely certain of the next step.

It has been more than a score of years since we had so many types from which to make a selection. Some fashion folk say that the ready-to-wear garment makers are purposely effecting extremes to dissatisfy women folk, and thus forcing more generous buying. This plan has been followed in dull business years or seasons to stimulate trade, but rarely is it so evident at the very outset of a new Fashion calendar.

The banker at this time says save, but the merchant insists that to keep industry's wheel turning one must empty the purse. The worthy word of both must be considered; hence, using great care in selection and buying cautiously will make possible thrifty saving, thus satisfying both merchant and banker.

The Basque is ever adored because of its truly feminine charm; the Empire, on petite figures, is generally approved because of its exquisite coquettishness; the Directoire is especially admired for its dignity. But the American woman seems ever to hold faithfully to the straight-line type of dress, because of its general becomingness and adaptiveness to her particular needs.

The straight-line type chosen for the first dress in this Service carries many of the new features and seems fashioned solely for the woman who likes one especially dainty dress for very special occasions.

Material and Pattern.—Your imagination will help you to visualize this dress made of dull violet-lavender crêpe de Chine with hand-drawn hemstitched panel lines and dainty ruffles finished with picot edging, or of gray crêpe de Chine, a color so fashionable now, or of white, flesh, or navy blue.

This same dress made up in beige voile with shadow embroidery in brown is delightful to see. Gray with rose or blue shadow or cross-stitch embroidery is also very pleasing. The color can be just what you like; but the material must be soft to emphasize the daintiness of the style.

If there is need for greater slenderness, all the ruffles may be omitted, a square- or V-neck effect used, and a very narrow "string of a belt" of self-material substituted for the sash.

And now before we talk of amounts of materials or of pattern or cutting, we must consider the skirt length. Nice dresses carefully made will carry over for second best next year, and the length must be made safe for that reason. One prominent fashion man says, "Tell all to use deep hems. They are not only fashionable, but safe." France has been trying for a year to introduce a longer skirt. Some of the shops are showing them, some fashion people are heralding them, but others say the short skirt will stay in until every woman and girl possesses at least one. Then they will go to the other extreme and have them as long and as narrow as possible.

The skirt length sanctioned by the best shops seems quite ladylike, for it is from 2 to 3½ inches longer than the skirt of the past winter; that is, 7 to 11 inches from the floor.

The cartoonists and the jesters give much attention to the youthfulness of our present-day fashions, ridiculing them in a half appreciative way. But none can decry the real charm in youthful costumes, even if the skirts are short, when they are dignified and becoming.

Six yards of 40-inch material is ample for the average figure. The reason for this quantity is the plaits at the sides and the panels, which are separate from the waist and hang over the skirt in apron effect. Because of the straight skirt, no pattern is required, and the plain foundation-waist pattern will prove entirely satisfactory for cutting the waist portion.

Cutting.—First cut the skirt, measuring three full skirt lengths, plus the hem, which should be 2¾ to 10 inches deep, the depth depending on individual preference and the amount of material available. Split one length through the center lengthwise, and thus provide the front and back skirt panels.

If you desire more fulness for deeper plaits than the two widths, or 80 inches, provide, use a scant extra half width at the back and arrange it so that the seams will come under the panel and be concealed by it.

Cut the waist very plain, placing both center back and front on a fold of material. Cut an opening at the left-side front, from a midway point on the shoulder. Then apply a narrow facing and an extension flap as in a wash placket, so as to make the opening inconspicuous under the panel. The neck of the waist portion should be shaped in a becoming way after the panels are in place in the fitting. And a word about neck lines. Becomingness, rather than Fashion, should ever be a guide to their development. This season neck lines seem trying at best, so great care should be exercised in adapting the fashionable ones. We should not find fashions impossible for us, for always we can modify them to a point of individual attractiveness.

Cut the waist panels the width of a scant chest measure, and make them 1½ inches longer than the waist portion measures from the shoulder line at the neck to the waist lines in front and back, respectively. Cut the ruffles on an exact crosswise thread and make them so that they will be 1⅛ to 1⅜ inches wide when finished and in place on the panels.

Construction.—Sew both skirt seams and press them open. Then put the hem in by hand, using easy, loose stitches so that the hem will not appear sewed. Hems must be more skilfully done now than ever before, for their chief charm seems centered upon the invisibleness of the stitches. Arrange the plaits, making ten or twelve ¼- to ½-inch plaits on each side, with ¾- to 1¼-inch spaces between. To determine on the size and spacing of the plaits, subtract the panel widths, less 8 inches, from the skirt width; divide the remainder equally, and divide this space into as many plaits as the amount will rightly make.

If the seam with the placket opening comes under the panel at the left-side front and the other under the panel at the right-side back, the location of the plaits will be easily determined. Baste them accurately, all on lengthwise threads, and then press them.

Next, plan to ornament the panels. If you are expert in making drawnwork, this will be very effective, but time is required to draw the threads, especially in silk, and to hemstitch. Very tiny, even cross-stitches varied at even distances by one large cross-stitch made with harmonizing or self-color thread is attractive; or, tiny hand-run pin tucks make a very smart and pleasing decoration. For Georgette or organdie, shadow embroidery in an attractive color provides an unusual trimming. Neatness and accuracy are the two considerations in ornamenting the panels. The pin tucks will prove easiest and safest for one not skilled in hand work.

Have the ruffles picoted on the edge or finish them with a rolled hem. Join them to the panels in a French seam, using a tiny pin tuck on the right side to hold the seam back and in position, or use a facing in hem effect. If the ruffles are omitted, then all the panels should carry hems 1½ to 2 inches deep on the sides and 6 to 12 inches deep at the bottom.

Join the foundation waist and the skirt to a stay belt, and attach the panels in fitting. Shape the neck edge of the panels as desired, binding the edges with a narrow bias binding and holding them in place with slip-stitches.

Cut the sash on a true bias 12 inches wide, using soft satin, taffeta, or self-material hemmed or picoted on all edges. Fasten it at the left-side front or finish it with a bow or a looped sash.

Model 12

Variations of Straight-Line Dress

Model 12A.—With straight lines evident in so many styles and fabrics of crêpe-like character and subdued luster heading the list of favored spring and summer materials, the generously proportioned woman may feel that her clothes problem is not such a trying one as it has been in many past seasons. Of course, there are any number of features and extremes that she must avoid if she would "put her best foot forward," but this caution must be observed in varying degrees by all types, for each individual, regardless of whether she is of stout, average, or slender build, must give due consideration to style selection in order that she may emphasize her very best points.

In this model, which, as illustrated, is suitable for the average large-proportioned woman, Canton crêpe in zinc gray is very simply trimmed with self-covered buttons and small embroidery motifs developed in silk floss of a slightly darker shade. The vest is formed of two rows of narrow, cream-colored lace arranged so that the scallops meet at the center.

For developing this style for the average figure, provide 4½ yards of 40-inch fabric, 1⅛ yards of crêpe de Chine, Georgette crêpe, or other light-weight silk in a matching or a contrasting color for facing the panels, ½ yard of lace about 2 inches wide, and 6 skeins of silk floss.

For each skirt panel, four in all, provide a straight strip of material about 10 inches wide and of the skirt length. For cutting the waist, use a plain foundation pattern on which are outlined the vest and the odd side-front seam line.

Model 12B.—Crêpe de Chine in Marion blue depends for its trimming on drawnwork and self-covered buttons in this model. The collar is of white batiste, pin-tucked and edged with Val insertion and lace. The cuffs are of self-material.

For the average figure, 5½ yards of 40-inch fabric is sufficient for making this model. A straight strip of batiste about 4 inches wide and ¾ yard long, 1 yard of insertion, and 1¼ yards of edging are required for the collar.

Form the pattern for the center-front waist panel, which is extended to form the sash ends that tie at the center back, by experimenting with muslin, pinning a straight thread of the muslin at the center front, cutting the panel as wide as you desire it, and letting the opposite grain of the material extend around the waist line.

In cutting the material, you may find it advantageous to make the overskirt and waist panel crosswise of the material. Study the arrangement of the pattern pieces very carefully before cutting any parts of the dress.

Make the hems in the overskirt sufficiently wide to extend to the first row of drawnwork.

Model 12C.—That youthful styles have no monopoly on novel ideas is illustrated by this model of tan-figured voile with seven overlapping skirt panels, six of which are pointed at the lower edge and give the effect of an overskirt with an uneven hem. Of the voile, 5 yards is sufficient for the average figure. Combined with this are a collar and a vest of white or ecru batiste, of which ¾ yard is required, and a sash of satin ribbon that matches in color the background of the voile, 2½ yards of material being needed for this.

For each of the pointed panels, cut straight strips 2 or 3 inches shorter than the skirt length and about 10 inches wide. Shape the lower edge of each of the strips as illustrated. For the back panel, cut a straight strip 12 or 14 inches wide and do not make this pointed at the lower edge.

Finish the edges of the panels with picoting, binding, or 1-inch hems whipped in position by hand. If the self-covered buttons were omitted, the hems used to finish the front and lower edges of each of the panels might be secured with machine hemstitching to provide a pleasing trimming.

Model 12D.—A one-piece dress having princesse lines was designed as a component part of this summer suit of silk serge in a soft pheasant shade. The lines of the dress, although suitable for the average figure, are rather severe for a slender person, but if made more nearly straight and the fulness held in at a low waist line by means of a wide sash, the complete costume would be an excellent one for this type. For the average figure, provide 5 yards of 40-inch fabric for this costume. For the collar, if it is to be made of contrasting material, supply ½ yard.

Cut the dress with the aid of a two-piece princesse pattern that is slightly fitted and has fulness gathered in the under-arm seam at the waist line. Make this in slip-over style with a faced slash at the center front.

For the jacket, use a pattern cut on slightly flaring box lines. Before applying the bias strips, mark the lines that you wish to follow, arranging these lines in the manner that will prove most becoming to the individual. In applying the bias pieces, slip-stitch them along both edges, being careful not to draw the stitches so tight as to cause any unevenness in the strips or to detract from their soft appearance.

Model 12E.—Blouses no longer follow the ordinary trend of style as they did for so many years. Instead, we look forward each season to real novelty as to both cut and trimming, for since the passing of the established rule that blouses must be confined by the skirt belt and not extend below the waist line, they have assumed an air of individuality that is truly delightful.

For tailored wear, blouses are not materially different from the styles that have been sanctioned for so many years. Such models are made of voile, dimity, wash satin, crêpe de Chine, radium silk, and similar serviceable fabrics. Low-neck styles in which the Peter Pan collar is predominant and plaited frills are used extensively, and high-collared models, more strictly tailored and with finely plaited fronts, are the principal types.

In the dressier models, Georgette crêpe, crêpe de Chine, Canton crêpe, tricolette, and a very few satins and taffetas are evident. Of these fabrics, Georgette crêpe is of leading interest.

Beaded and embroidered designs are used in abundance on these models. Much of the embroidery is in all-over designs of the scroll kind or distinctively of peasant influence in the color schemes as well as the motifs that are employed.

Crêpe de Chine in a medium-bright shade of orange is the material used for this costume-blouse with its "fly-away" sash, a feature that has brought blouses and dresses into closer relationship. The plaited frill, also, is of crêpe de Chine, and the collar and cuffs are of white organdie embroidered in orange. For the average figure, 2 yards of crêpe de Chine and 1¾ yards of embroidered organdie are required.

In cutting out the blouse, use a semifitted basque pattern having set-in or kimono sleeves, according to your preference. In making the blouse, secure the sash ends in the under-arm seams.

Model 12F.—There seems to be no diminution in the vogue for combinations of fabrics. This feature is evident in blouses as well as dresses, and not only suggests unusual effects with the use of two materials but also affords opportunities for utilizing remnants or for remodeling.

This two-fabric blouse has chosen Robin's-egg blue Georgette crêpe for its foundation and crêpe meteor in pearl gray embroidered in blue for its cuffs, back panel, and front trimming bands. For the average figure, 1½ yards of 40-inch fabric is needed for the foundation and sash and ½ to ⅝ yard for the trimming.

Cut the back panel and the front trimming bands of straight strips of material. Make the bands for the front about 3½ inches wide, when finished. Use a slightly flared pattern for cutting the cuff and finish the outer edges of all the crêpe-meteor sections with picoting or face them with Georgette crêpe.

12 D

12 B

12 A

12 E

12 F

12 C

Bloused Sash Dress

A very much glorified sash is claiming our attention this year—so important has its use become that its absence seems to be the exception rather than the rule. We are bewildered to note the extremes to which a sash will go to make itself the center of attraction on Fashion's stage. Some sashes are content to be little wider than string girdles, others are 4 to 6 inches wide and merely tied once, leaving the two sash ends but no loops, and still others are as wide as 10 or 12 inches and not satisfied merely with sash ends, but insist on a "fly-away" bow of no modest dimensions. There is a like amount of diversity in the position where a sash may be tied to be strictly up to date. The sash that is tied at the side just in front of the under-arm seam and is generally worn on a bloused dress is probably the feature of the season; the one tied at the center back is its close second. There are any number of departures from these positions, for, according to the design, the side back, the center side, and even the center front of dresses having rather classic lines seem the most desirable.

The vogue for sashes may owe much of its prominence to the bloused dress, for a sash seems to provide just the right finish for such a style. Almost invariably the waist line is dropped below normal when a bloused effect is used, and a sash draped below this and looped at the side suggests the Spanish influence, which is receiving so much consideration at present.

Bloused effects are not generally becoming to the stout figure, but if the effect is made less prominent and the collar and sash narrower, this design would serve for the average stout person.

A word about the embroidery on the blouse—this is in eyelet effect, but is used in only a very moderate degree as compared with the extensive use of this embroidery on many styles. If worked skilfully, it is very attractive, but otherwise it might better be omitted or an easier embroidery stitch substituted.

Material and Pattern.—A notable feature of this dress is the fact that it is made entirely of one fabric and in one color. The material is Canton crêpe; the color is eucalyptus, a soft, medium-dark green. Almost any of the medium-weight spring silks, such as crêpe de Chine, crêpe meteor, soft taffeta, or pongee, may be selected. Even a fine, soft quality of serge would prove suitable if the sash were made of silk.

Provide for the average figure about 4¾ yards of 40-inch material, ½ yard of net or 1 yard of China silk or lawn for the waist lining, and from 3 to 8 skeins of floss, depending on the kind of embroidery you intend to use.

No skirt pattern is necessary, for the skirt is made of straight sections of material that are steam-plaited. A plain-waist pattern having a slightly deepened armhole and an extension below the waist line for the bloused effect, a collar that may be attached to the normal neck line so that it rolls back with the fronts, and a slightly flared cuff pattern are all that are required.

Cutting.—For the skirt, cut two widths of material, making each of them the desired skirt length, plus allowance for a hem.

Place the back waist, sleeve, cuff, and collar patterns as suggested for the cutting of the plain blouse that is considered in the dressmaking lessons. Place the front portion of the waist so that the center front is 4 or 5 inches from the edge to allow for the slightly rolled effect and the front facings.

Try arranging these pattern pieces in various ways in order to determine the most economical method of cutting the material. If possible, cut the sash in one strip along the selvage, making it 2 or 2¼ yards long and about 6 inches wide. If you find it more advantageous, cut it crosswise of the material in two strips or on a true bias to provide the number of strips that will give the required length. The bias sash is no longer a necessity, for on many frocks the sash is cut lengthwise or crosswise.

Construction and Fitting.—First, in preparation for the steam plaiting, form the right-side skirt seam, stitching this only once and pressing the seam open. Do not seam the left side; this must be left open so that the material may be laid out flat in the plaiting. Then, determine how long you wish to make the skirt, turn the hem, and slip-stitch it in position with comparatively loose stitches. Also, determine how wide the panel should be made to prove most becoming and baste the lines for the panel on the front-skirt section. Then have the skirt plaited.

Next, make and fit the lining, attach it to a soft, loose inside stay belt, pulling the lining down well on the figure, and supply both lining and belting with hooks and eyes. Baste the blouse and sleeve seams, turn back the fronts about 1 inch beyond the center-front line so as to form the facings, and baste these turned edges in position. Then fit the blouse and sleeves, noting the points suggested for the plain blouse. After removing the blouse, stitch the seams and, with the exception of those at the armhole, press them open; press back the edges of the armhole seam together so that they extend into the waist rather than into the sleeve. Then gather the waist line of the blouse.

Finish the upper edge of the piece provided for the vest with a narrow bias binding or a 1-inch hem, or face the vest with light-weight silk. Make the double collar as suggested for making a similar collar for the plain blouse. Make the cuffs in practically the same manner, but before stitching the cuff and the facing together join each of them with a plain, pressed-open seam, making sure that they will fit the lower edge of the sleeve properly. Also, if you wish to embroider the cuff, do this before applying the facing. Then apply the embroidery to the blouse.

Make the skirt ready for the fitting by removing, near the left-side opening, the stitches that secure the hem, opening out the hem, and then stitching a seam at the inside edge of one of the plaits to within 8 or 10 inches of the waist line, exercising care in doing this work to make the plaits appear even and the hem as if continuous on the right side. Then fold the hem back in position over the seam line and secure it with slip-stitching. Finish the opening in the seam with a narrow binding. Then, with the plaits folded in position, gather the waist line.

Next, put the lining and belting on the figure and pin the vest in position; then put on the blouse, roll back the fronts, as illustrated, and adjust and pin the waist-line fulness to the stay belt, letting it blouse as much as you desire. Also, pin the collar and cuffs in position. Adjust and pin the fulness of the back and right front of the skirt to the stay belt, and secure to a bias binding the left front, which extends from the center-front opening of the waist to the skirt placket. A steam-plaited skirt must be "hung" from the waist line instead of from the hem; therefore, if the skirt appears uneven, drop or raise it at the waist line until it hangs evenly. Draw the sash around the figure and place pins at the points where you wish the ends looped.

Finishing.—Baste and stitch the waist and skirt to the prepared belting. Also, baste and stitch the collar and cuffs in position, finishing them as directed for the application of the collar and cuffs of the plain blouse. Then secure the right edge of the vest to the lining and tack the right front of the waist to this.

Finish the raw edges of the blouse at the left-front waist line by clipping them rather close to the stitching and covering them with a narrow bias facing.

Face the sash ends that extend beyond the pins with self-material, and face the remainder of the sash, or the part that extends around the waist, with China silk. If the material is light-weight silk, the sash may be made double of self-material.

Complete the dress by tacking the sash in position, sewing ½-inch, self-covered buttons to the center front of the skirt panel, and securing snap fasteners along the blouse and skirt openings.

Model 13

Variations of Bloused Sash Dress

Model 13A.—For some time there has been talk of the cape coat and cape suit and even of the separate shoulder cape to be worn with a one-piece dress, but the abbreviated cape that is really a part of the dress is a novelty of distinction. This cape effect, as shown, bears a semblance to the Eton, but it is a trifle longer and fuller. White and jade-green crêpe de Chine with embroidery in jade and black and a sash of black ciré ribbon were used for this model.

The design is one that might be copied in linen or ratine, but if made of either of these materials it should not be embroidered so elaborately.

For the average figure are required 3 yards of material 40 inches wide, 1⅜ yards of contrasting material of the same width, 20 skeins of silk floss, and 1½ yards of ribbon.

Form the pattern for the cape effect with the aid of the plain-waist pattern, using this to shape the neck and shoulder lines. Extend the lines straight from the end of the shoulder; then, to provide a slight ripple, slash the pattern at one or two points from the lower edge almost to the top and separate the pieces sufficiently to produce the flare you desire. To secure the cape in position, slip-stitch it to the neck and shoulder lines of the blouse. Make the trimming bands of the skirt, sleeves, and cape double. Also, make the collar double, cutting this from a pattern formed by experimenting with muslin.

Model 13B.—Daintiness in the superlative degree is expressed by this flesh-colored Georgette-crêpe dress. The trimming is of chalk-white beads and appliqué roses made of self-material. A recurrence of the bloused effect and the bound slash in the waist is noted in the skirt, which is finished in Turkish fashion. The bands that trim the skirt are cut lengthwise of the material and made double. They are secured at the side front under the sash; then they are permitted to fall just below the skirt at the side and are brought up to the hip line at the side back. A small dart placed at the inside edge of the band at the point where this is looped and concealed by the beaded design provides the shaping that is necessary.

Material requirements for the average figure are 6½ yards of Georgette crêpe and about 20 bunches of beads. This estimate of Georgette includes an amount sufficient for a camisole waist lining and also for an underskirt to be used as a foundation to which the fulness of the outer skirt may be applied.

Model 13C.—There was a time when the use of straight pieces of material for trimming purposes was as decidedly out of the question as a skirt made without goring. A comparison of some of the old-time styles, intricate as to design and trimming, with a model such as this, which is typical of the straight lines and simplicity evident in present-day fashions, makes one deeply appreciate Dame Fashion's indulgence of our desires.

The model is of crêpe de Chine, anemone in color, with white crêpe-de-Chine trimmings. Lengthwise strips cut 6 inches wide and then doubled are applied to the skirt by securing the two raw edges of the strip in a tuck or a French-seam effect that is evident only on the wrong side of the skirt. When the dress is on the figure, the free or folded edge of the strip naturally drops and extends below the skirt hem, thus producing the uneven effect that marks the design as strictly up to date.

The yoke effect in the skirt may be made as an extension of the waist or cut separate and applied after the trimming strips have been secured to the lower portion of the skirt. The sash is cut about 7 inches wide, faced with white crêpe de Chine, and draped with the facing turned back at the upper edge.

Voile or organdie in two plain, harmonizing colors would be an excellent substitute for the crêpe de Chine. Of the one color, 4½ yards of 40-inch fabric, and of the color for trimming, 1¼ yards of material, are required for the average figure.

Model 13D.—Strictly of an afternoon type is this dress of Georgette in a colorful tan, sometimes referred to as bran, combined with cream-colored filet lace and a sash of bright-green satin. For the average figure, 7¼ yards of filet insertion 8 or 9 inches wide, 3½ yards of Georgette crêpe, and 1 yard of satin or 2½ yards of ribbon for the sash are required.

To form the skirt drapery, use a straight strip of lace edged with double lengthwise bands of Georgette that, when finished, are about 1½ inches wide. Cut these strips in one length from the piece of Georgette that has been provided. Apply this lace-and-Georgette band by extending it from the side-front waist line to the skirt hem, looping it at the bottom, and then bringing it up to the waist line at the side back. Tack the upper center of the loop to the side of the skirt, as illustrated.

For the lining of the dress, cut a camisole of Georgette with a vest effect of the filet. Make the back panel of a strip of insertion and join it to the side sections. Then, to simulate a separate back panel, edge it with double lengthwise folds of Georgette, leaving the folded edge free. Make the collar of a double lengthwise strip of Georgette and tack this in position.

Model 13E.—There is decided smartness in the high-collared dresses that are coming into prominence. And to wear one is to experience a very much "dressed-up" feeling that is just a bit different from the effect produced by the average dress intended for only occasional use. A commendable feature in this collar is that it may also be worn low, as in (a), as the taste of the wearer may dictate. In no case should it be buttoned over the throat if it serves unpleasantly to accentuate the shape or fulness of the face, for an unbecoming neck finish is liable to influence the entire design and make the dress unsatisfactory.

What more apropos color than "Mrs. Harding" blue could have been chosen for this model of soft charmeuse? Silver-gray satin is used for the sleeve and collar facings, as well as for the front-waist facings, which are folded back on the right side to form a binding or vestee effect. The silk-floss embroidery, also, is of silver gray and the buttons are of steel. For the average figure, a design such as this requires 5 yards of charmeuse, ⅓ yard of satin, and 15 skeins of floss.

Before attempting to cut the blouse portion of this design, cut at least the upper portion of the front and back in muslin, leaving on the front an extension of sufficient size for the front collar portion, but marking the neck line of the front portion. Then join the seams of this model, put it on the figure, and carefully fit the front portion in at the neck line, arranging for a seam at the center side. Also, fit in a back collar portion. To form the collar facing, fit a piece of muslin over the collar portion after you have removed the muslin model. Make this in one piece with a natural neck line marked from the blouse.

Form a pattern for the skirt draperies by experimenting with muslin. Let the longer portions of the drapery be on the lengthwise of the fabric, and arrange for a seam at the center side or for seams at each side of the flared portion.

Model 13F.—Combinations of gray and gold are among the most pleasing of the season's selections. This model of gray crêpe de Chine has a collar of soft-gold satin and chain-stitch silk floss embroidery of gold and black. The buttons that accentuate the slot seam at the front are self-covered.

Only 4 yards of crêpe de Chine is required for making this model for the average figure. For the collar, ⅜ yard of satin should be provided, and for the embroidery, 12 skeins of floss, 8 of gold, and 4 of black.

Cut the waist as a plain-kimono bloused style, and the skirt of straight pieces of material. In addition to the front seam of the skirt, provide seams at the sides. These will be made less conspicuous by the application of the embroidery.

15A

15B

15C

15D

15E

15F

(a)

2

Tunic Dress

Dame Fashion has such a charming way of luring us each season into the acceptance of seemingly new styles that we are often accused by thoughtless, and perhaps envious, masculine minds of submitting to her absolute domination. Such propaganda as this in the age of republics! With the deepest respect for Fashion's authority and all due credit to her ingenuity, we must disclaim a servile attitude.

No longer do we all don styles of the same general character at precisely the same time. Instead, we demand a certain degree of comfort and adherence to lines that we have found most becoming, and Fashion, realizing that we are thinking for ourselves and that we are hesitant about dropping a satisfactory present-day feature for an uncertain, even though enticing, new idea, caters to our preferences and conceives all sorts of ways for us to follow them without appearing in the least passée.

This, and possibly no better reason on earth, can account for the continued vogue of the tunic dress. The great majority of us have worn it and liked it and therefore have continued to wear it. And if we take such a charming model as this as typical of the new tunic dresses, we realize how very dependent on our inclinations Dame Fashion has become.

This season a different touch is provided in the charming manner in which she drops the tunic below the hem line of the underskirt and thus centers interest at this point. Uneven hem lines are really the whim of the hour and are so easily achieved in tunic dresses.

As illustrated, this style is suitable for slender and average figures. The uneven tunic effect, however, is becoming to a stout person and, with a waist having long lines, might be used to form an appropriate costume.

Material and Pattern.—Fine voile of soft jade, one of spring's delightful colors, is the material used for this model. Perhaps the fact that jade is becoming only to certain types brought into the designer's mind the thought that such a color should be used without stint whenever it is permitted at all, and so the shadow lace, which was selected for the trimming, was chosen in a color to match the voile. The waist-line finish consists of a sash of matching satin ribbon tied at the side.

For cutting this dress for the average figure, 5 yards of voile and 6½ yards of lace 6 inches wide are necessary, and for the waist lining ½ yard of fine net is required. In addition, 3 yards of 8-inch ribbon is required for the sash.

Plain waist, sleeve, and two-piece straight-skirt patterns with a few slight changes may be used for the development of this style.

Prepare the waist pattern for use by outlining the broad neck line on the front and back portions. Also, turn the lower portion of the sleeve and skirt patterns back to make them of the length you desire them when finished, taking into consideration the fact that it is not necessary for the skirt material to extend under the lace. Also, if the skirt pattern is wider than you desire, fold in the extra width. At the present time, a skirt used under a tunic is generally made about 1½ yards in width for the average figure.

Form the tunic pattern by experimenting with muslin, letting a lengthwise thread form the lower edge of the tunic, dropping the material at the side waist line to form the pointed effect, and curving the waist line as much as you find necessary. Cut the side line on a decided bias.

In cutting the material, place the center front and back of the tunic pattern on a crosswise fold. At the lower edge of the skirt, provide an allowance of 1½ or 2 inches, to make possible any slight change in length you may desire in the fitting.

Shape the neck line of the lining as for a corset cover, and arrange the opening at the left shoulder and under arm.

Construction.—Join the sleeve seams, the under-arm and shoulder seams of the blouse, and the side seams of the tunic and skirt as French fells. Leave the left skirt seam open at the upper edge and finish this as a bound placket. Then baste the lace to the lower edge of the tunic and the skirt. To form the double-sleeve effect, turn a hem that is half the width of the lace and then baste the lace along the upper edge of the inside of the hem. In order to make an attractive finish at the sides of the tunic, try to arrange the lace miter so that the pattern of the lace matches exactly or as closely as possible. Merely pin the miters in position before fitting the dress. Also, gather the waist line of the tunic and skirt, starting the gathering at the left side seam and letting the ends of the gathering threads free to permit of their adjustment when the dress is being fitted.

Fitting.—Secure the inside stay belt in position on the figure, so that the closing is at the left side. Then put on the net lining and adjust and pin the fulness to the stay belt. Also, adjust and pin the fulness of the skirt to the stay belting, and, if necessary, change the position of the lace on the underskirt in order to produce an even line at the lower edge. Next, put the blouse on the figure and pin the lace in position to form the yoke effect at the front and back. Try arranging the lace on a practically straight, or horizontal, line from shoulder to shoulder, and then form a neck line more nearly round in order to determine which effect is more becoming. If you decide that a round neck line is more becoming, it will be necessary to gather in the fulness that results at the upper edge and secure this with a narrower binding than the one illustrated. For a horizontal neck line, provide a double bias binding that will be about 1¼ inches wide when finished. Fit this in position with the folded edge at the top and pin it securely. Be sure to keep the neck line sufficiently large to permit the blouse to be slipped over the head.

Next, adjust and pin the fulness of the tunic to the blouse portion, and make sure that the mitered-lace corners are of the same length and extend the same distance below the skirt.

Finishing.—Stitch the lace in position, taking this stitching along the upper edge, with the exception of the strips in the blouse portion, which should be stitched just above the lower scalloped edge. If you prefer, you may have the lace in the sleeves, tunic, and skirt secured with machine hemstitching. Cut away the material under the lace in the blouse portion to within a seam's width of the stitching, and finish this edge, as well as the edges under the remaining lace joinings, by turning them under and securing them with fine whipping-stitches. Finish the bias strips at the neck line by turning both edges to the inside and securing the lace between these edges with stitching or machine hemstitching. Then join the shoulder seams of the blouse, and insert the sleeves with French seams or bound plain seams.

In order to make a neat finish at the waist line of the blouse and tunic portion, which is made entirely separate from the waist lining and underskirt, stitch the blouse and the tunic together, bringing the seam edges to the right side. Then trim the seam edges quite close and cover the seam with a bias facing about ⅜ inch wide. Through the casing that is formed in this manner, run an elastic that is of the same length as the inside stay belt. This will hold the fulness in position when the dress is on the figure.

Complete the dress by sewing snap fasteners the entire length of the under-arm closing of the lining and underskirt and just one fastener at the shoulder closing of the lining. Last of all, make the ribbon sash, tying the bow so that it will not be necessary to untie it each time the dress is removed and securing it merely at the under arm. Finish the end of the ribbon at the waist line and sew on a snap fastener to secure it to the bow.

Model 14

Variations of Tunic Dress

Model 14A.—Voile has been a long-standing favorite for summer frocks, perhaps because it has such a satisfying way of retaining its fresh appearance for many more hours' wear than the average summer fabric. Among the very newest of voile weaves, as shown in this model, is that having a ratine stripe, a suggestion borrowed from the revival of ratine as a sports fabric. The color is a rather bright tan, caramel by name. Quite unusual in effect are the straight bands of a lighter tan linen used to bind the center-front opening of the waist and tunic. Linen also is employed for the entire underskirt, the cuffs, the sash, and the collar. The design requires, for the average figure, 2¾ yards of voile and 2½ yards of linen.

As illustrated, the design is suitable for average or slender figures. Made with set-in sleeves and with the trimming bands continued to a longer neck line, it would prove becoming to a woman of rather large proportions.

For the waist of this dress, use a kimono-waist pattern that has a seam running through the shoulder and center of the sleeve, and in cutting, arrange the seam as far toward the front as you wish it. Cut the lengthwise strips for the trimming bands from the pieces taken from the sides of the lengths used for the skirt. Make these 3 inches wide, so that when applied, they will be about 1¼ inches wide.

Model 14B.—When a dress is made of two materials, it generally creates a twofold interest. Not only are carefully selected combinations of materials almost invariably pleasing, but they also offer excellent possibilities for disguising last year's frock and thus effect considerable saving.

This model, as illustrated, is of figured Georgette and taffeta, the Georgette in brown and nasturtium tones and the taffeta in a rich, harmonizing brown. Much of the smartness of the design may be credited to the open effect above the vest and the narrow ribbon tied at the center front to give a suggestion of a higher neck line. The vest is of bands of cream-colored filet-lace insertion. For the average figure, 3 yards of Georgette crêpe, 3 yards of taffeta, and ¾ yard of filet lace about 4 inches wide are required.

As an early spring or a midsummer style, this design would prove equally pleasing. For the former, it may be made of taffeta and serge; for the latter, of voile and organdie.

Cut the pointed sections 12 to 15 inches deep and determine their width by dividing the width of the tunic by the number of sections you wish to apply. The sash may be made of lengthwise strips of material taken from the sides of the skirt lengths.

Model 14C.—To have just one tunic is to be ordinary, according to the idea of some of the very newest dresses whose skirts are covered with a series of tunics. And so eager are these dresses to emphasize their favor for "tunic piled on tunic" that they insist on the waist being unobtrusive in design.

Crêpe de Chine in a soft, medium shade of blue, with bias bindings of self-material, buttons self-covered, and a sash of blue-and-gold plaid ribbon with silk-tasseled ends that extend below the skirt hem leave little that one who boasts of youth or slenderness could desire. With care exercised in the cutting, 5 yards of crêpe de Chine will prove sufficient, provided the upper part of the underskirt is made of China silk or some light-weight lining fabric. The sash requires 2½ yards of ribbon.

For midsummer wear, handkerchief linen would be an excellent material, or if you prefer the crêpe, choose white and make the sash and bindings of black ciré ribbon.

Form the tunic sections of straight pieces of material. Let the underskirt extend about 2 inches up under the widest tunic portion, which should extend to the waist line.

The upstanding collar may be made of a double, straight strip of material that is about 1 inch wide when finished.

Model 14D.—Swisses having colored backgrounds and white or contrasting colored dots made their appearance last summer, but the supply was so very limited that only the early purchasers were fortunate enough to procure them. The rest of us, although disappointed because we had to resort to white Swiss, were hopeful that another season would bring an abundance of colors. Now our hopes are more than realized, for the shops have an excellent showing of the loveliest colors imaginable.

In this model, yellow Swiss is combined with white organdie—a combination whose very appearance on a hot summer's day is bound to prove almost as refreshing as an icy drink.

The apron tunic, a feature evidenced in so many spring designs, and the loose back panels permit of a profusion of organdie bindings. The bindings are used also for finishing the sash, collar, vest, and cuff edges.

A style such as this requires, for the average figure, 5 yards of dotted Swiss and 1½ yards of organdie.

Colored organdie might be combined with eyelet batiste for this same style. For a spring dress, black taffeta could be used without contrasting material in the apron, and the collar, vest, and cuffs made of red-and-white checked gingham—a startling fad for this season—or a pastel-color checked dimity.

Make the apron portion of a straight piece of material about 36 inches wide, and the panels of straight strips 9 inches wide.

Model 14E.—To find a style that is "different" and yet suitable in every detail for the mature or stout woman—seemingly, what a task! And yet, this very model evidences all these features. The material is figured voile having a conservative design in which gray predominates. The trimming bands, which are looped under the skirt hem, are of plain gray voile, and, this same material is used for the underskirt and vest. The neck line is softened by a collar of white batiste edged with Val lace and insertion. Turn-back cuffs of the same material finish the long sleeves. If gray is especially becoming, this may be used in place of the batiste.

For the average stout figure, 4¼ yards of figured voile, 2¾ yards of plain voile, ⅜ yard of batiste, 2¼ yards of insertion, and 3 yards of edging are required.

Cut the trimming bands lengthwise of the material. Make them double and about 2 inches wide when finished.

Model 14F.—Summer and organdie—these terms have become practically synonymous, for what is summer without organdie frocks in their delicate, as well as dashing, colors so suggestive of garden flowers from the most demure of tea roses to the brilliant gladioli? From such a range of colors, orchid was chosen for this youthful model. Soft rose and blue ribbons were used for the narrow sash effect, and white net with Val insertion and lace trimming was employed for the vest and sleeve finish.

Material requirements for developing this design for the average figure are 6 yards of organdie, ¼ yard of net, 1¼ yards of insertion, 1½ yards of lace, and 3 yards of each kind of ribbon.

As a graduation dress, this model would be lovely in white organdie, and for evening wear or class night, chiffon or taffeta might be chosen.

The tunic of this dress is formed of two straight pieces of material. To form the distended or loop effect at the waist line, bind the side waist-line edges with self-material or have these edges picoted; then tack the edges to the waist line at points about 7 inches apart, permitting the material in the spaces between to extend out, as illustrated.

Apply the rows of lace and insertion to the vest before gathering the fulness into the neck-line binding. Finish the collar and the lower edge of the tunic with bias bindings that, when finished, are about ⅜ inch wide.

14A

14B

14E

14F

14C

14D

Waist-Line Dress

For some time past, a conscientious effort to keep posted as to the correct position for the waist line has been no less difficult than trying to determine the authoritative length and width of skirts. Opinions have varied and shifted to the extent that almost any position for the waist line has been accepted, provided it has not ventured above the natural waist line. And now there is even wider latitude permitted, for both Mid-Victorian and Directoire influences are receiving considerable attention, and the high waist line is a feature of these periods.

What degree of importance may be attached to the advent of the high waist line is a point difficult to determine at present. Certainly it is winsome and youthful when worn by the proper type of person, but it holds little of interest for the well-developed or stout figure and must, therefore, depend on the youthful type for any impetus it may gain.

The lowered waist line continues to be one of Fashion's outstanding features, but the normal waist line also comes in for a goodly share of favor, for there is a conservatism about it that is generally appealing.

Material and Pattern.—In this model, rust-colored crêpe de Chine and a figured crêpe de Chine in which rust color predominates are combined in a manner typical of the season's use of two fabrics. Whereas, in seasons past, the general plan has been to use the plain material for the foundation and the figured fabric for the overdress or trimmings, just the reverse of this method is now followed.

The same principle is also carried out in the use of embroidery. For instance, this model might be made entirely of one material and an all-over embroidery design applied to the vest, the panel front, and the lower edge of the skirt, thus suggesting an embroidered foundation.

For the average figure, 3¾ yards of plain material 40 inches wide and 2¼ yards of figured fabric of the same width are required for the development of this model.

A plain two-piece skirt pattern, a one-piece sleeve pattern, a waist on which a vest is outlined, and a collar in narrow roll style are all that are required for the cutting of this model. To make the narrow roll-collar pattern, experiment with muslin. Let a straight thread of the material extend along each side of the vest portion and shape the collar around the neck line, making it roll as much as you desire. Form a bias seam line at the center back, and trim the collar to make it about 2 inches wide through the lengthwise portion.

Cutting.—For each of the accordion-plaited tiered sections of the skirt, cut two widths of material from which have been cut lengthwise strips 5 inches wide for binding the front edges of the tiered sections. Make these tiers of the length you desire plus allowance for finishing. They may be finished with a picoted edge or with a 2-inch hem.

Place the waist and sleeve patterns on the material in the usual manner. Then consider the arrangement of the collar pattern. This should be placed on the material exactly as it was cut in the muslin, and a facing of self-material should be provided for it. For the sleeve frills, cut straight pieces twice the sleeve width and as deep as you desire them. Then cut out the skirt and vest portions.

Construction.—First of all, prepare the sections cut for the tiers and sleeve frills for plaiting. Join the sections provided for each skirt tier, and then hem one edge of each tier or have the edges picoted, whichever method is more convenient. Prepare the strips cut for the cuffs in a similar manner, but turn a narrower hem on these. Then send the material to be plaited and proceed with the construction of the dress.

Join the waist, sleeve, and skirt seams in the usual manner, and after making sure that no change is required in the seam lines, finish them as French fells.

Make the collar by joining the bias center-back edges of the upper portion, as well as the facing, with a plain pressed-open seam. Then place the right sides of these two portions together, stitch around the outer edges, and turn the collar right side out.

Prepare for the principal fitting of the dress by making the waist lining, if you wish one, finishing the stay belt with hooks and eyes, and gathering the waist line of both the blouse and the skirt and also the unfinished edges of the plaited sections.

Fitting.—Adjust and pin the waist-line fulness of the blouse and skirt to the stay belt, and turn the hem in the skirt. Then pin the plaited tiers in position, arranging the lower tier so that its upper edge is well covered by the upper tier. Use an abundance of pins in this fitting, so as to insure correct results in the finishing, and do not be satisfied with the appearance of the skirt until the tiers hang on a perfectly even line that is parallel with the lower edge.

With the tiers properly arranged in position, pin the skirt trimming bands in place. These should be applied double, to form a binding for the front edges of the tiers. Pin these bands to the skirt as well as to the edges of the tiers. In order to provide an opening in the skirt, slash it just under the inner edge of the band applied to the left side.

Pin the vest in position in the waist; then pin the collar in place. Also, turn the lower edge of the sleeve to make it the length you desire and pin the frill in position.

Finishing.—Replace by fine basting-stitches the pins that were used in the fitting. Then stitch the fulness of the blouse, skirt, and upper tier to the stay belting as it was pinned in the fitting, and stitch the lower tier flat to the skirt. Cover the raw edge of this lower tier with a narrow facing of self-material.

Finish the opening in the skirt by making a bound placket. Cut the hem an even width all around and secure this with fine, loose whipping-stitches. Secure the skirt bands by first slipping one edge under the edge of the tiers, stitching flat to the skirt the edge of the tiers as well as the band, and then turning the upper edge of the band under and securing the edge by means of slip-stitching over the row of stitching first made. The outer, or folded, edge of a band applied in this manner will be free from the skirt and will provide a very soft effect. Finish the lower end of each band by turning the raw edges to the inside and slip-stitching them together.

Apply the collar by stitching the facing to the blouse, then turning the edges of each of these inside of the collar, turning the raw edge of the upper collar portion under, and slip-stitching this over the row of stitching that secures the facing. Finish the upper and left edges of the vest by hemming them, make a narrow turn to the right side on the right edge of the vest, and stitch this to the blouse. Stitch the sleeve frills in position, and cover the raw edges with a narrow facing.

Clip the raw edges at the waist line close to the row of stitching, and cover them with a narrow bias facing. Then, if you wish to copy the waist-line finish that is illustrated, make the belt of a double lengthwise strip of material cut long enough to extend in an easy manner from one side front around the waist line to the opposite side front, adding 2 inches for finishing. Tack the belt in position at two or three points and connect the ends with large beads and a novelty ornament that harmonizes with the dress fabric. If you are unable to procure a suitable ornament, use a narrow ribbon sash.

Complete the dress by applying snap fasteners along the side-front opening of the blouse and the placket opening of the skirt.

Model 15

Variations of Waist-Line Dress

Model 15A.—That a dress may be entirely neutral in effect and still be of marked interest is proved conclusively by this lovely afternoon or evening model of silver-gray Georgette crêpe with trimming of glass beads and filet lace in self-color and a sash of mauve ribbon in a very soft faille weave. The long lines of the dress, combined with the dignity of which the materials and trimmings are suggestive, make the model especially desirable for the woman whose age and inclinations are such that she is satisfied only with designs of a distinctive, matronly nature. If the dress is intended for a stout woman, the use of a self-colored sash without loops will be better.

Voile in white or a light color might be used for this dress, and machine-hemstitched hems, rather than beads, employed for finishing the edges. For the average figure, provide 4 yards of Georgette crêpe, 1⅛ yards of lace insertion about 15 inches wide, 1 yard of matching insertion 2¼ or 3 inches wide, 3 yards of ribbon, and 3 bunches of beads.

In making this dress, join the skirt portion with plain seams; then turn the seam edges away from the panel, roll the material out over the seam line on the right side just a trifle, and apply the beads to hold the material in this manner. Finish the remainder of the edges to which the beads are applied by securing narrow hems with the stitches that hold the beads.

Model 15B.—An innovation, rather than a revival, in style features is bound to be of momentous interest and is especially worthy of this interest when it assumes a form so lovely as the petal frocks that are claiming attention at present. Although such frocks are made in a variety of materials, they appear at their very best when a sheer, pastel-colored fabric is employed, thus making their resemblance closer to the flower petals from which the name is derived.

Strictly of an afternoon type or for summer evening wear is this model of chiffon in tea-rose pink combined with delicate cream-colored lace and finished at the waist line with old-blue satin ribbon that is fastened at the side with a cluster of roses. For the average figure, provide 5 yards of chiffon, 5 yards of lace 10 to 12 inches wide, and 1 yard of 6-inch satin ribbon.

Apparently, the development of a skirt such as this involves a number of intricate details, but in reality it is quite simple. Make the underskirt of two straight pieces of material, one of which is several inches wider than the other so that the seams, instead of falling at the center sides where they would be evident, will be concealed under the drapery of the lace.

For each of the petals, six in all, a straight strip of material 3 or 4 inches longer than the skirt length and about 12 inches wide is required. Before cutting these strips, indicate the division lines by means of basting and have these lines, as well as the outside edges, machine-hemstitched. Then cut the hemstitching to form lengthwise picoted edges for all the strips.

Apply the petal at the right-side front first, pinning it in position when the dress is on the figure. Place the strip so that its lower edge is even with the bottom of the skirt and its left edge extends 1 or 2 inches to the left of the center front of the skirt. Then slant the left edge up to a point 1 or 2 inches to the right of the center front, letting the surplus extend above the waist line, and pin the left edge of the strip to the skirt.

Next, to form the cascade effect, let about 8 inches of the upper edge drop at the right side and lay the fulness under this in plaits that will extend into cascade folds. The lower right corner will naturally fall below the hem, but to make this point even more decided, cut away the lower edge from a point on the left side of the strip 2 or 3 inches above the bottom of the skirt on a slanting line to the right corner. Have this edge, as well as the upper edge of the cascade portion, picoted. Then tack the left edge of the strip in position and apply the remainder of the strips for petals, letting one overlap the other.

To make the lace drapery for each side, use a strip that is twice the skirt length, plus 4 or 5 inches. Apply this by extending it from the lower edge of the skirt at the side front to the lower edge at the side back, taking up the surplus at the center by folding it in plaits in the manner illustrated. The scalloped edge of the lace will naturally fall in cascades and extend below the skirt hem in pointed effect.

Model 15C.—Shadow lace is applied in a very simple manner, but with unusual and pleasing effect, in this model of fine white voile. Hand-hemstitched drawn work, a feature that seems to show partiality to voile, relieves the severity of the blouse portion, and in harmony with this feature, the mitered corners of the lace are finished with machine-hemstitching. Black ciré ribbon adds a striking contrast as a waist-line finish. Besides tying around the waist line in the usual manner, it achieves distinction by means of a series of plaited rosettes. Georgette or crêpe de Chine might be substituted for the voile if a more elaborate dress is desired.

Provide for the average figure 3¼ yards of material 40 inches wide, 12 yards of 6- or 7-inch lace, 2 yards of matching lace, and 4 yards of ribbon about 1 inch wide.

The waist portion of the dress is extended several inches below the waist line and the skirt attached at this lowered line. The mitered-lace corners are formed by leaving a 3- or 4-inch allowance on each end of the lace and then seaming the lace from the lower corner on a decidedly diagonal line to the upper edge of the lace when it is attached. If the opening at the neck line is not large enough to permit the dress to be slipped on and off with ease, additional length may be provided by arranging an opening on the left shoulder.

Model 15D.—When a fabric is accorded such universal popularity as is now being shown for white crêpe de Chine, it is certainly justified in choosing for its design features that serve merely to emphasize its beauty. Accordion plaiting provides one way of accentuating the loveliness of crêpe de Chine. And what more appealing use can accordion plaiting find than in an overdress? A mere suggestion of color is afforded in this model by a beaded rose design applied to the sash.

To develop this model for the average figure, 6½ yards of material and 2 bunches of beads are required. This amount makes sufficient allowance for deep hems in the skirt and overdress. Make the foundation waist in plain kimono style, and add the plaited waist sections as separate panels, binding these at the neck line with self-material. Make the skirt portion of the overdress separate, letting it extend all around the figure.

Model 15E.—The fact that foulards are going to enjoy another season of popularity is well demonstrated by the ready sale of this fabric, which has been promoted by the attractive shop displays. Foulard has a twofold attraction at this time, for it is typically a spring silk and, besides, carries with it a well-established reputation for service.

A very wide tuck in this model of foulard gives a suggestion of a long tunic. Especially worthy of note is the back opening, in this case filled in with strips of embroidered batiste like that used for the cuffs. In many models that show this back opening, it is made a trifle shorter and left open except at the neck line, where the edges are held together with a bow of ribbon or self-material. Horizontal darts placed at the front armholes of the blouse portion afford a means of providing a little extra fulness and thus make the lines a little less severe.

For the average figure, provide 5½ yards of 36- or 40-inch material for this model. This will prove sufficient for a 10-inch hem and a 12-inch tuck. For the trimming, provide 1½ yards of narrow batiste embroidery and 2½ yards of narrow ribbon.

15a

15c

15b

15d

15e

One-Piece Dress

Another proof that Fashion cooperates with her followers rather than dictates to them is evident in the continued vogue of the one-piece dress. There is something charmingly youthful about a style that does not define the curves of the figure, and this very concealment of curves is likewise flattering to the stout woman, provided the dress is designed on long, conservative lines. For instance, kimono sleeves must be avoided unless broad panel effects are supplied in the front and back of the waist portion, for the omission of the armhole lines or panel or overblouse lines has a tendency to emphasize the thickness of the shoulders. Also, the shaping of the neck line is of importance in the designing of a dress for a stout person. To prevent the appearance of thickness in the neck, the dress should be brought up close at the sides.

Straight sections of material skilfully applied can do much toward lifting a plain one-piece dress out of the ordinary class, as this model very forcefully illustrates. The foundation of this dress is a simple, kimono slip-over style with a horizontal dart just below the waist line extending from the side front to the side seam. This dart makes it possible for the skirt to hang on straight lines and not fall toward the front. Also, it permits extra fulness in the skirt without a flaring under-arm line, for this fulness may be gathered into the dart line.

Typical of many of the spring styles, the straight side panels of this design extend below the skirt. The straight back panel differs from a similarly placed panel that was so popular last season in its abbreviated length.

Material and Pattern.—As illustrated, this model is made of brick-colored crêpe de Chine with embroidery of self-colored silk floss and metallic silver thread, and the vestee and revers facings are of gray satin. Provide for the average figure about 5¾ yards of crêpe de Chine, ⅜ yard of satin, 1 dozen skeins of silk floss, and 8 skeins of silver thread. Panels of the kind used on this dress are very often lined throughout with Georgette crêpe or satin in self-color, or contrasting color.

Use a one-piece kimono-dress pattern for cutting the foundation of this design, and make this with a normal neck line, leaving the shaping to be done in the fitting. Make allowance for the 12-inch hem when cutting the skirt portion.

For the side panels, cut straight strips long enough to extend from the point you desire above the waist line to a point about 2 inches below the skirt hem, plus an allowance of 3 inches for the finish at the upper and lower edges, making these strips, for the average figure, 16 or 17 inches wide. This width will provide 1-inch hems on the sides of the panel. Cut the back panel 1 yard or more in length and 15 inches wide, this estimate also including allowance for hems. Very little work should be done on this dress before the foundation is carefully fitted.

First Fitting.—In preparation for this fitting, gather the lower dart edge and then turn under the upper dart edge, tapering this turn from the beginning of the dart, and baste it with short, firm stitches over the gathered portion. Then baste the under-arm seam edges. At the center front of the dress, make a slash from the neck line about 6 inches long, being careful to cut this on a lengthwise thread and just deep enough to permit the dress to be slipped over the head with ease.

Put the dress on and observe the manner in which it fits over the shoulders and at the under arm. Also, notice whether or not the skirt seems to hang correctly from the waist line. If the dress seems very baggy at the under arms, pin in the extra fulness. Keep in mind the fact, however, that a dress of this kind should be very "roomy" and hang on practically straight lines. If the skirt appears to fall toward the front, try lifting it at the dart line, and pin the new seam.

Construction.—Before stitching the under-arm lines of the dress, proceed to finish the dart. Stitch the dart from the right side of the material, following the turned edge closely. Then finish the dart by taking a few over-and-over stitches on the wrong side, just under the point where it begins, in order to strengthen it and prevent it from tearing out.

Next, join the under-arm edges by means of plain seams; press these open and overcast them. It will be well to reinforce these seams through the curved portion where the sleeve starts. For this purpose, use a bias strip of material 3 or 4 inches long and about ⅜ inch wide with both edges turned. Place this over the stitched seam line and stitch this on both edges flat to the pressed-open seam.

Next, turn and baste 1-inch hems on the sides and lower edges of the back panel portion and along the sides of the side panels. At the lower edge of the side panels, baste hems about 2 inches wide, and at the upper edge, turn under about ½ inch and baste or press this edge.

Second Fitting.—Put the dress on the figure and turn the hem at the lower edge. Then turn the fronts back at the neck line to form the revers, shape the neck and revers, and slash the center front deeper, if you desire. Also, mark the lines on which you wish the hemstitching done for the lower edge and the slashed portions of the sleeves.

Next, pin the back panel in position so that it is even with the neck line of the dress, and after making sure that the panel hangs properly, mark or trim the panel neck line to make it even with the edge underneath. Then pin the side panels in position, arranging them as shown in the illustration, so that the side-back edges just meet the edges of the back panel. Observe whether or not the side panels extend an even distance from the skirt hem, and make any adjustment that may be necessary. A slight change may be made by lifting or dropping the upper edge of the panel and then forming an even upper line; a more decided change may require adjustment at both the upper and the lower edge.

Finishing.—Secure the side panels to the garment by turning them back and stitching across the upper edge on the creased line indicating the edge that was turned in the fitting. Stitching done in this manner will not be evident when the panels are turned back in their correct position. Secure the hems in the skirt and panel edges by means of close, but rather loose, whipping-stitches.

Baste the facing for the revers in place with its wrong side over the wrong side of the dress; then have the edges of the revers hemstitched. At the same time, have the hemstitching done on the section for the vestee and on the sleeves. Secure the inner edge of the revers facings with invisible whipping-stitches and tack the right edge of the vest in position.

Now, a precaution in regard to sewing buttons on material as soft and yielding as crêpe de Chine may be needed. Draw the stitches just close enough to hold the buttons in position properly. Tight stitches will cause the crêpe de Chine to pucker and make the work appear amateurish. Do not break the thread after securing each button; rather, continue this on the wrong side of the garment or inside of the panel hems to the point marked for the next button. Then take two or three tiny backstitches at this point before securing a button over it, so as to prevent the weight of the buttons from drawing the thread that connects them.

Make the sash of straight strips of material that, when seamed together and doubled, will be about 1 inch wide and 2½ yards long. Tack this in position at two or three points, and arrange the ends so that they may be tied at the left side.

Model 16

Look for a collectible print version at the end of this issue.

Variations of One-Piece Dress

Model 16A.—How fortunate is the girl or woman of average type—the type for whom the big majority of styles are designed. For her, extremes in styles are not prohibitive; in fact, there are few style features that are unbecoming to her and therefore she may, as a general rule, select just what appeals to her most strongly, provided, of course, it is suitable for the purpose she wishes. Only an average type should adopt this style, for the narrow trimming bands at the back and the front make the lines too long for a slender person, and the shape of the neck line, the kimono sleeves, and the shoulder fulness make it undesirable for the stout figure.

Blue taffeta and fine serge, as this design illustrates, a fur or fabric neckpiece, and long kid gloves suggest a charming street costume for late spring, when the days are too warm for a suit or top-coat and yet the season is not sufficiently advanced to make summer frocks appear in good taste. The serge is used for the lower skirt portion, the trimming bands at the center front and back, the very abbreviated shoulder yokes, and the cuffs and sleeve trimming bands. Of this material 54 inches wide, 1 yard is sufficient, and of the taffeta, which is used for the remainder of the design, 2¼ yards is required.

As a guide in cutting the dress, use a kimono one-piece dress pattern having a shoulder seam extending through the sleeve; on this, outline the band at the lower edge of the skirt. In the cutting, allow a little fulness at the shoulder. Form the shoulder yoke of a straight section of material that, when finished, is about 3 inches wide and extends 3 inches from the neck edge. Make the cuff straight and about 3 inches wide, and extend the center of this on a straight grain to the shoulder yoke in the form of a band about 2 inches wide.

Hold in the fulness at the under arm by means of corded shirrings. Do not, however, draw the dress in very close to the waist line; rather, permit it to blouse just a trifle and otherwise hang on practically straight lines.

Model 16B.—The vogue for eyelet embroidery, although regarded with varying degrees of approval, certainly should win popular favor when it is thought of in eyelet batiste, for here it appears to the best advantage, because of the airiness and daintiness it imparts to this typically summer fabric. In this instance, the batiste is of a lovely ecru shade that harmonizes with the tan crêpe de Chine used for the front and back skirt portions, the under-arm waist portions, the sleeves, and the neck band. Material requirements are 2¼ yards of batiste 36 inches wide, and 2 yards of crêpe de Chine.

Crêpe de Chine with figured Georgette crêpe, figured voile with plain voile, and checked gingham with chambray of a harmonizing color suggest other possibilities for this design. A plain one-piece dress pattern cut on a line denoting the division of the materials may likewise be used. To mark this line properly, hold the dress pattern on the figure and chalk the lines as the divisions are illustrated.

Cut the flaring side portions of the dress the full skirt length. Make these about 12 inches wide at the lower edge and let them taper to a point at the waist line. Cut the under-arm of the crêpe absolutely straight, letting all the flare be provided by the sections of embroidered batiste. Outline the front and back bands for the neck finish on the one-piece dress pattern. Secure these bands before joining the waist seams by first placing them over the wrong side of the batiste, neck edges even, stitching on the seam line, turning the bands to the right side, turning under the free edges, and then stitching or slip-stitching them down.

Join the upper section of batiste to the crêpe by turning under the edge of the crêpe and stitching it flat to the batiste, or, if you prefer, you may have this joining hemstitched. Join the skirt by means of French seams or plain seams with the edges turned back on the crêpe and bound together.

Model 16C.—No degree of comfort is sacrificed in this very pleasing design, and yet its every detail is expressive of smartness. The straight silhouette is maintained even though the skirt has ample width provided by the inverted plaits at the sides. The line of the raglan sleeve is unusual; for most figures, such a sleeve in a one-piece dress can be made to fit better and to prove more comfortable than a kimono sleeve.

The desirability of this design is increased by the materials used, Canton crêpe of a platinum shade choosing the same material in blue for trimming and the points being outlined in metallic silver. The girdle is of blue wooden beads, a novelty of merit.

For the average figure, 3 yards of gray crêpe and 2 yards of blue will prove sufficient. If the points are outlined with a darning-stitch, 15 yards of the silver thread will be enough.

Form the pattern for the skirt trimming by marking the points on the foundation pattern, measuring carefully so as to make all these points of the same size and the spaces of equal depth. Let the side line of the skirt pattern, or the plait edge, form the straight edge of the trimming section. In cutting the trimming, make the usual seam allowance at the sides, and at the lower edge make allowance for a hem.

Cut the under portions for the inverted plaits separate from the front and back skirt sections. Then, before joining these portions for the plaits, secure the trimming in position on the front and back skirt sections.

Model 16D.—Isn't there a certain youthful appeal in a Peter Pan collar or one cut on similar lines? New York shop showings are a proof of this, for what but youth could inspire the use of this collar on so many different designs? Vestees are often used with these collars, and generally both the vestee and the collar are finished with bindings of contrasting or self-material, as this design shows.

The dress is of wool jersey in a new shade of blue that is medium as to tone and rather bright as to character, the vestee, collar, and cuffs are of white linen, and the trimming bands, of a rather heavy novelty cotton tape about 1 inch wide. For the average figure, 3½ yards of jersey and ½ yard of satin are sufficient for the dress. If five rows of tape are applied to each side of the skirt and another row is used to outline the vest edge, 10 yards of tape will be required. In applying the tape, stitch it flat on both edges.

A model of this kind is very attractive if made of white wool jersey with trimming of navy-blue tape or of white crêpe de Chine with black or henna ciré ribbon substituted for the tape. It might also be developed in linen or plain gingham.

Model 16E.—Long lines should not prove boresome even to the woman who has had to consider them for many years, provided these lines are achieved in such an interesting way as by the insertion of elongated gussets of contrasting material. The collar, while not unusual in design, is made interesting by its trimming of knife-plaited frills. Far better is a becoming collar that is not of a new variety than are the broad curves of some of the recent designs that require a very shallow V neck line and are therefore anything but flattering to the stout person.

Heralding the popularity that is predicted for brown linen, this model is certain to win instant favor. The long inserted sections, the collar, and the plaited frills are of ecru voile, 1¼ yards being required with 3½ yards of linen. The drop-crochet buttons are of ecru and the belt is of ecru leather.

Cut this dress as a plain one-piece style, and in the first fitting mark the lines for slashing at each side of the front and back; also, determine whether or not you wish to take out any of the fulness before the contrasting sections are inserted. These sections may be made as inverted box plaits to give ample freedom in the skirt.

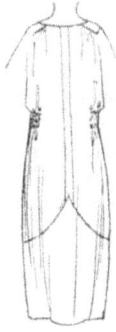

16 A

16 B

16 C

16 D

16 E

Basque Dress

When the occasion comes to arrange for a bridal gown, all preciseness in sewing is set aside. Custom and sentiment, rather than Fashion, seem ever to decide the style, and romance, rather than technique, to direct the energies of the needle.

Shimmery satin, lace, and a mist of tulle emphasize the romanticness of the bride's gown. It is said that these fabrics have held sway throughout centuries because of their definite feminineness. This may also be said of the basque type of bridal gown, the basque lines seeming ever right for such a dress and occasion. This feature is pleasingly youthful and appears to excellent advantage when made in crushed and semifitted effect in combination with a draped skirt, as in the design illustrated. The draperies of the skirt are at each side back, merely a suggestion of them being evident on the front.

Material and Pattern.—Provide for the average figure 5 yards of satin and 2 yards of lace 5 inches wide with ¾ yard of matching lace 8 to 10 inches wide. For lining the train, 2 yards of Georgette crêpe or chiffon is required.

Before cutting the basque of the dress, outline the positions for the lace on a long-waisted, semifitted basque pattern. In cutting, leave a generous seam allowance above the line marked for the lace, so that you may make any change you desire in the fitting. No pattern is required for cutting the skirt, as this must be shaped in the draping. For the train, cut a piece of full-width material, making this about 2 yards long, or longer if you have provided extra material for this purpose.

Construction.—First of all, make a straight waist lining or slip of light-weight silk, cutting this high enough to provide arm-holes and long enough to extend almost to the knee, so that it may also serve as a foundation for the drapery and make a stay belt unnecessary. Arrange for the closing of this at the center back, so that it will be in line with the skirt seam.

Next, baste the lace in position at the upper edge of the front and back basque sections. Then join the right under-arm seam of the blouse, leaving the left under-arm seam open so that the closing may be arranged at this point.

Fitting and Draping.—In order to drape the skirt becomingly, first put the lining on the figure and secure it in position; then take the straight piece provided for the skirt and pin its cross-wise center at the center front of the lining several inches below the normal waist line. Draw the ends of the material around to the center back, pinning in the fulness at the side waist line and forming the drapery at each side back by looping the material down from the waist line and then drawing it up at the center back and arranging the folds as illustrated. Pin a seam at the center back, making this as decidedly bias as seems necessary to give ample fulness through the upper portion and make the skirt the width you desire at the lower edge.

Before removing the dress, tack the drapery inconspicuously at the points where such stitches seem necessary. Also, put on the basque and take care of any fitting or rearrangement of the lace that is advisable and turn under the lower edge. Cut away the silk under the lace, leaving a seam allowance. Then replace this with fine net or flesh-colored chiffon so as to provide a filmier appearance. You may let this foundation extend close to the scalloped edge of the lace or cut it in corset-cover effect; in either case, the edge should be picoted.

Finishing.—Stitch the seam at the center back of the skirt, leaving this open at the upper edge and finishing it with an inconspicuous bound placket. Also, secure the upper edge of the skirt to the lining, making any slight adjustment of the fulness that seems advisable.

Secure the lace to the upper portion of the basque by turning the satin over the lower edge of the lace and slip-stitching it in position. Then finish the satin portion of the armholes with narrow facings held in place by invisible stitches. Instead of facing the lace, roll and whip the edges with extremely fine thread or have these edges picoted. Face the left under-arm edges of the waist.

Make the train ready for application by turning under 3 or 4 inches at each side and at the lower edge, and then slip-stitching the facing of chiffon or Georgette crêpe in position so that it covers only a seam's width of the edges of the satin.

Again, put the dress on the figure. Pin the lace in position at the lower edge of the bodice, drawing the ends up under the lower edge at each side back, as the illustration shows. Next, mark the line for turning the lower edge of the skirt. Then pin the train in position at the back waist line, distributing the fulness carefully.

In removing the dress, observe the manner in which the closing must be arranged. At the waist line, the lace, bodice, train, and skirt must be finished separately from the center back to the left under arm, for the opening of the skirt and of the lining is at the center back.

With the dress removed from the figure, secure the lower edge of the bodice and the lace to the skirt and lining by means of slip-stitching, taking these stitches well up under the folded edge, so that they will not detract from the softness of the finish. Face the lower edge of the skirt with chiffon or Georgette crêpe and use the greatest of care in securing this facing in order not to take the stitches through to the right side.

Complete the dress by securing small snap fasteners at all points where they are necessary. Use these as sparingly as possible, but in sufficient number to make the closing secure, and apply them cautiously so that there will be no evidence of them on the right side of the dress. A long cluster of white roses may be dropped from the waist line at the side, as illustrated.

Model 17A.—When a bridesmaid is attired in a frock of corn-flower blue taffeta and white organdie or chiffon designed on quaint, winsome lines and trimmed unstintedly with rosettes of Val lace, her charm all but eclipses that of the bride. The collar with its unusual arrangement of lace, which is applied in all-over fashion, is finished at the center front with a cluster of roses in colors that blend very pleasingly with the corn-flower blue of the taffeta. The extreme fulness of the crisp taffeta skirt is responsible for the distended-hip effect, while the rather closely fitted basque further accentuates this.

To develop this dress exactly as illustrated for the average figure, provide 4 yards of taffeta, 1 yard of organdie, and 30 yards of Val lace. In cutting the bodice, use a pattern that has a three-piece back and a one-piece front, and provide sufficient length in the bodice to permit it to be crushed in softly at the waist line.

For the skirt, use a full-width piece of taffeta from 2 to 2½ yards long and gather this along one lengthwise edge, thus making it up crosswise of the material in order to dispense with seams. Make the inserted front panel of a straight strip of organdie about 20 inches wide. Stitch this to the taffeta by means of a plain seam, and then fold the taffeta back over the organdie to form a plait effect about 2 inches wide and give the organdie panel the semblance of a foundation skirt.

Make the foundation for the collar of organdie and that for the rosettes of net. Cut the rosette foundation circular and have the edges picoted. Apply the lace after drawing up a thread in the edge so as to make the lace slightly full, starting at the center of the foundation and arranging the rows as illustrated, so that one just overlaps another.

Model 17

17a

Variations of Basque Dress

Model 17B.—To win popular favor this season, a foulard need not be printed in novel or intricate design, for polka dots and coin spots are now considered the very essence of smartness. In many instances, the dots provide a decided color contrast; in other cases, the colors are rather closely related and prevent the dots from being brought out in such bold relief.

A very pleasing color combination is noted in this model; the background of the foulard is of navy blue and the dots of henna. Straight picoted bands of Georgette crêpe in a color that matches the dots are used in such abundance on the overskirt that little of the foulard is evident in this part of the dress. A repetition of this trimming serves to give character to the otherwise plain sleeve. In place of the vestee of cream-colored satin, Georgette like that used for trimming may be employed, if desired.

Of the foulard, about 5 yards will be required for the average figure. For the trimming bands, 1¼ yards of Georgette crêpe should be provided.

Figured material is not really essential for this design. It might be made of plain-colored crêpe meteor, crêpe de Chine, or Canton crêpe, and bands of a contrasting color in the same or contrasting fabric employed for trimming.

Before cutting the material provided for the trimming bands, mark on it the lines for hemstitching. Make the spaces between the lines equal to twice the width you desire the trimming bands; then after the hemstitching is done, cut on the hemstitched lines to form the picoted edges and also cut through the center of each picoted strip. The unfinished edge of each of these strips will be concealed in the application of the bands.

Model 17C.—When a petal frock is made of a fabric that has as much body as taffeta, a foundation skirt is not necessary, provided the petals are held together to form a complete skirt, as in this beige-colored model. The edges of the petals are bound with self-material. Besides the slip-stitching that holds the petals together, tiny tailored bows of ribbon, which have a decorative value that is youthful and in nowise ordinary, are applied to give added firmness. In place of ribbon, small bows of self-material may be employed with pleasing results.

The basque effect is one that is particularly becoming to a slender person, for the soft fulness provided by the corded shirrings at each side front and the deep cut of the neck line filled in with a vestee of organdie relieve the severe and closely fitting effect that is charactertistic of many basque models. The neck line is finished with an embroidered organdie edging, and a touch of this appears again in the sleeve.

For the average figure, provide 3¾ yards of taffeta, or of organdie, if you prefer, for the model is one for which this fabric is suitable. For the neck and sleeve finish, provide 1⅜ yards of narrow organdie embroidery, and if you wish to make the little bows of ribbon, provide about 5 yards of a ¾-inch width for this purpose.

Make each of the skirt petals about 9 inches wide, if you wish to make eight petals, and form the scalloped effect by rounding the lower corners of each of the strips. Arrange the closing of the dress at the left shoulder and under-arm seam.

Model 17D.—When bright red as a color for wear in warm weather made its initial appearance last summer, it was considered by many as a mere passing fad or fancy that would have only a short season's duration and not receive any notable attention in even so short a period. It may have been the designer's skill, or, on the other hand, the surprising attractiveness of this color in sheer summery fabrics, usually combined with white, that gave such an impetus to its popularity. At any rate, red is here in such force that already there is talk of a coming scarcity of all the fabrics in which it predominates.

Without following any extremes in regard to red, this model of gingham or tissue gives evidence of its progressive ideas by the broadness of the red stripes with which the white background is plaided. Double bands of white organdie are applied to the skirt in such a manner as to give the effect of separate panels. The folded edges of these strips are finished with narrow bands of organdie arranged in points, as illustrated on the collar, and the opposite points held together with tiny, washable-organdie buttons, thus giving an interlaced effect at the sides. The buttons are also used along the shoulder seams of the collar.

For the average figure, 3½ yards of gingham, 1¼ yards of organdie, and 4 dozen organdie-covered buttons are required for the development of this model.

Cut the skirt of this dress in two pieces, arranging the seams at the center sides so that they will be at least partly concealed by the pointed organdie trimming.

Form the pattern for the odd collar by experimenting with muslin. Cut it with a lengthwise thread at the center front and center back and a seam on each shoulder.

Model 17E.—In this model, a series of ruffles of self-material is arranged to give a panel effect at each side front of the very full skirt. Another interesting feature of the dress is the manner in which the sections of the semifitted basque are shaped in scalloped effect at the lower edge. Canary-colored organdie, which is delightfully refreshing both as to color and fabric, is used for the dress, and white organdie trimmed with lace edging, for the collar and cuffs. The ribbon sash is of a medium-bright shade of blue, in pleasing contrast with the yellow, and is charmingly finished where it ties at the side with an artificial rose in shades of yellow.

As a class-night dress, this style would be quite appropriate. It might be made of either organdie or taffeta, according to the kind of material favored by the class as a whole. For the average figure, 4 yards of organdie or taffeta will be sufficient; for the collar and cuffs, ⅜ yard of organdie and 2 yards of edging will be required; and for the sash, 3 yards of ribbon 1 or 1½ inches wide.

In cutting the basque, use a semifitting pattern that has side-front and side-back seam lines; then shape the lower edge to make it individually becoming. Finish the seams with machine hemstitching or fine cording, and follow this method of finishing the lower edge where it is joined to the straight gathered skirt. Secure the ruffles with machine hemstitching, provided this is used for finishing the seams in the basque portion. Otherwise, place them so that the right side of each ruffle faces the right side of the skirt, with the picoted edge uppermost and the gathered edge of the ruffle directly over the line marked for its application, stitch on the gathered line, turn the ruffle down over the raw edge, and press it flat along the upper portion just over the stitching, so that it will not have a tendency to stand out from the skirt as it might otherwise.

Model 17F.—The intricacies of draped effects fade into insignificance in this season of handkerchief draperies, for what could be simpler or more interesting than the arrangement of squares of material at the sides of the skirt and on the sleeves of this model? The squares used on the skirt are made 10 inches on a side, finished with picoted edges, and applied so that one overlaps another, as illustrated, by securing merely one corner of each square to the skirt and permitting the remainder of the square to hang in soft folds over the one just below. Three squares, each 8 inches on a side, are used for the sleeve finish.

Crêpe de Chine is one of the loveliest and most satisfactory materials that can be employed for handkerchief draperies. For this model, which is made entirely of crêpe de Chine in steel gray, 5 yards of the fabric is required.

17 B

17 D

17 C

17 E

17 F

Magic Pattern: *Chemise Dress*

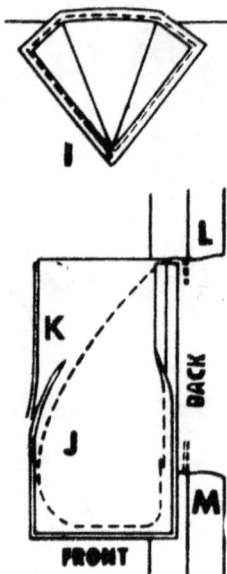

▶▶▶ THIS DRESS requires just one length (shoulder to desired length plus hem) of 54-in. fabric, or two lengths of 40-in. swaggerish gingham, such as was used for the model illustrated. Average requirement 2¾ yds., plus 3 yds. of seam binding and spool of thread.

Straighten fabric. If two lengths are used, cut or tear in half crosswise. Fold piece for front lengthwise, folding it over to a depth of one-fourth bust measure-ment plus 2 in., with fold toward you. Keep lengthwise grain straight on fold. Cut off any surplus width. This is used for pockets, sash, or added sleeve length.

Locate point A at left end of fold, as in the diagram. Mark B at one-fourth neck measurement above A; and C, one-half neck measurement to right. For shoulder slope, mark D 1½ in. to right of edge, as shown. To right of D measure one-half armhole measurement plus 2 in. for E. Pockets are inserted in side seams.

Mark F for top of pocket 6 in. below waistline. Mark G 6 in. below F. Measure 9 in. from bottom (right-hand edge) for side slits, and mark H. Cut from B to D.

Fold back piece lengthwise as for front. Place front over back and cut shoulder line B to D as on front. On front, cut on fold from A to C for front neckline.

Lay right sides of front and back together and stitch ½-in. shoulder seams. Stitch side seams from E to F and from G to H.

Put dress on. Lengthen neck opening if desired. Tie a cord around waist. Adjust fullness. Decide most becoming length. Turn bottom edges for hem on straight crosswise grain, both back and front. Adjust any variance in length at waistline.

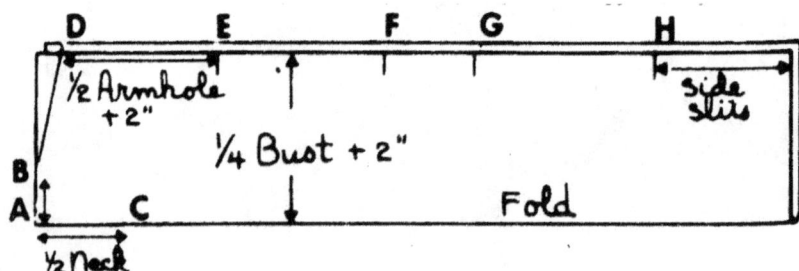

Remove dress. Put hem in. Slip-stitch along edge of side slits, so that finish will be neat. Finish sleeves and neck with seam binding, terminating binding at bottom of neck, as at *I* (wrong side).

Fold neck edge to wrong side, forming V, as shown. Slip-stitch in position around neck.

Cut four pocket pieces 10 in. long and about 6 in. wide. Seam two pocket pieces together, tapering from top to bottom and along bottom end, as at *J*. Trim off surplus, as at *K*.

Stitch one edge of pocket to front seam allowance, making ¼-in. seam. Clip back seam allowance, as at *L* and *M*. Stitch back edge of pocket to back seam. Repeat for other pocket. Tack seam top and bottom to prevent tearing out.

Put dress on. Adjust fullness under belt.

Your Measurement Chart & Notes on Making Magic Patterns

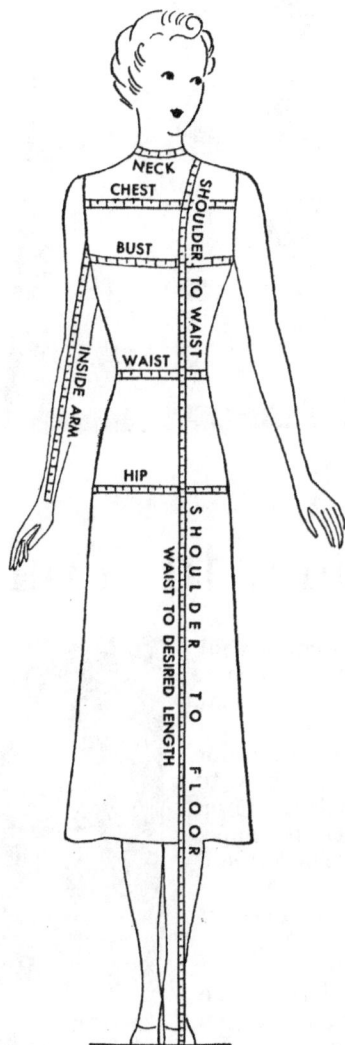

BUST (Fullest Part)............_____

WAIST ...._____

HIP (Fullest Part) ...._____

WIDTH OF CHEST............._____

FRONT WAIST LENGTH
Shoulder to Waist............._____

FRONT SKIRT LENGTH
Waist to Desired Length........._____

FRONT FULL LENGTH
Shoulder to Floor ...._____

NECK (At Base) ...._____

SHOULDER
Neck to Armhole Line..........._____

ARMHOLE ...._____

WIDTH OF BACK ...._____

BACK LENGTH
Neck to Waist ...._____

BACK LENGTH
Neck to Floor.................._____

OUTSIDE ARM
Shoulder to Wrist (Arm Bent)...._____

INSIDE ARM
Armhole to Wrist (Arm Straight) .._____

UPPER ARM (Fullest Part)......._____

ELBOW (Arm Bent) ...._____

WRIST ...._____

HAND (Closed) ...._____

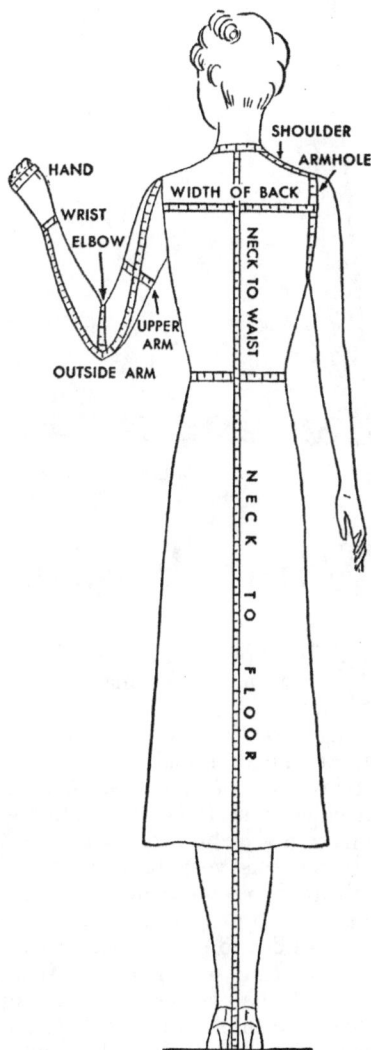

Keep Accurate Measurements

Since the garments in this book are all cut from measurements, it is necessary to have accurate ones to follow. Keep a list of your own measurements always at hand for ready reference.

Measurements for fitted garments should be taken over the type of foundation garments you expect to wear with them. Remove dress, jacket, or coat, which would distort the measurements. Do not take measurements too tight. Make all easy enough for comfort. The chart shows how to place the tape correctly for each measurement.

Making The Pattern

If you have the least doubt about your ability to chalk out the garment on your fabric, then rough it out first with crayon or heavy pencil on wrapping paper or newspaper. Cut out the paper pattern and use it to cut your garment. Cutting from a diagram, you can be sure that the proportions are correct for your size and that the garment will be a good fit.

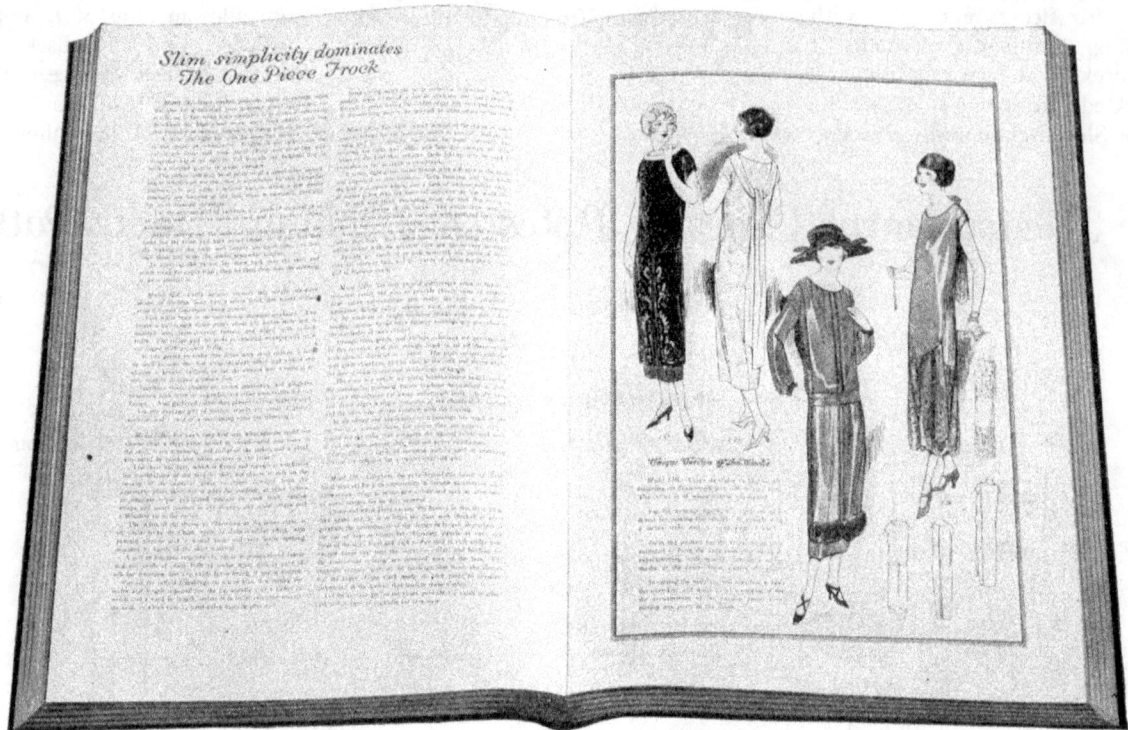

Two typical pages of Fashion Service—the Woman's Institute's own fashion book.

What Fashion Service Means to You

EACH approaching season in the world of dress brings a bewildering array of new fashion designs. It is little wonder that the woman seeking a distinctive or becoming dress for herself, or the dressmaker striving to express the individuality of her customer, goes from one magazine or style book to another vainly trying to make a selection from the profusion of models.

It was this very problem that prompted the Institute to create a new kind of service for its students. It presents four times a year through its own publication—Fashion Service—a discriminating selection of the choicest models of the best designers, all in one brilliant fashion display between the covers of one superb style book. For each of these models it presents several variations.

And then it tells you just how to make for yourself the design of your choice—what pattern to buy, what materials to use, what fabrics and colors are most appropriate in developing it for your particular type, how to handle the material, lay it on the pattern, cut it out, drape, fit, and finish it, and how to add those little touches of embroidery or trimming that make it distinctive.

Think what it means to have such a service coming to you *every* season. No wonder that students write us such letters as those below.

Fashion Service tells just how to make a smart costume like this at a third its cost in the shops

Fashion Service always contains many charming simple dresses for girls as well as grown-ups

Never Anything So Complete

I wish to thank you for the Fashion Service. Ever since I have been old enough to take an interest in the subject I have bought fashion books and tried to use them, but in all the years I can truthfully say I have never seen anything so complete in every way.

MRS. A. A. CONKEY, JR., Hudson, N. Y

Never Before So Much Distinction

I have gone through and through the beautiful Fashion Service Book, page by page, and each time I find something new to delight me. Each costume has so much individuality. I never saw so much distinction in dress assembled before.

MISS SUDIE L. LEE, Oklahoma City, Okla.

Like the Most Exclusive Shops

May I tell you how very much I appreciate the Fashion Book? It is quite the loveliest collection of fashions I have ever seen between two covers. It seems to be an unfortunate fact that even in the best publications only a few of the models are really consistently good. Only in the most exclusive shops here have I seen garments that appealed to me as do yours in Fashion Service.

MURIEL IVES OBRIG, New York City, N. Y.

Explains Just How to Make

I thank you so much for the Fashion Service. It differs so much from any other magazine or style book; you can never be in doubt as to how a dress should be made—it fully explains all.

MRS. G. L. WHELDEN, 1309 Grant St., Brunswick, Ga.

Originally published in "How You Can Have More and Prettier Clothes" Book, 1925

You Receive Personal Sympathetic Help of Women Who Are Interested in You

WHEN you join the Woman's Institute you are doing more than purchasing a course of instruction that will bring you the ability to make smart becoming clothes. You are becoming a student of a great educational institution, whose success has been built on the intimate, personal help it has been able to give to its students. You are forming an acquaintance with a group of earnest, sympathetic women who are masters in their profession and who have the teacher's eagerness to pass on to their students the skill in their art and the inspiration and enthusiasm for it which they themselves possess. You are coming in contact with women who will take a sympathetic interest in your problems and who will strive earnestly to help you get the greatest possible benefit from your course and your association with the Woman's Institute.

These women are thoroughly in love with their work. They recognize the need for a better knowledge of the home arts. They know the value of the courses they are teaching. They have seen thousands of women come to the Institute for help with their clothes problems, their home problems, and their problem of earning a livelihood. They have worked with these women, guiding their progress from lesson to lesson. They have rejoiced with them over their triumphs. They have seen thousands of them complete their courses and graduate. And from thousands of others they have had letters of appreciation and gratitude for the help which the Institute has given. They have experienced the joy of helping women better to prepare themselves to meet the responsibilities of life. They have felt the thrill of actually helping women to help themselves.

So when you join the Woman's Institute, you are making the acquaintance of women who are thoroughly imbued with the spirit of helpfulness and who will take a personal interest in you. They will ask you to tell them something about yourself, your circumstances, your needs, your experience in sewing, if you have had any, and what, in particular, you are most desirous of learning to do. With this information to guide them, they will strive to give you, as quickly as possible, just the help and training your circumstances and needs require.

The members of our staff wish you to consider them, first of all, as *your friends*. For that is exactly what they strive to be to every Institute student. They wish you always to feel free to write to them about your problems. They will consider your relations with them as confidential as would your most intimate friend. You can hand a letter to your postman or drop it into a convenient mail box with the confidence that it will receive the personal, sympathetic attention of a real friend who is interested in your welfare and whose aim is to help you in every way she can.

Some of our choicest friendships have grown out of our relations with our students. And from your welcome as a student, all through your course, we shall strive to put into our letters, our criticisms on your lessons, and all of our relations with you a cordiality and an interest that will make you realize that in the members of the Institute staff you have real friends. We want you to feel that joining the Woman's Institute was one of the wisest, most profitable, and most satisfactory things you ever did.

Originally published in "How You Can Have More and Prettier Clothes" Book, 1925

You Will Save Money by Remodeling Your Out-of-Style Clothes

CONSIDER your present wardrobe. Think it over, garment for garment. How many clothes have you hanging in your closet which you seldom or never wear? How many are in really good condition, only definitely out-of-style? How many are just in *fair* condition—not exactly too bad to wear, but not really up-to-date and becoming?

Do you realize what a waste these clothes constitute in your yearly expenses? Not only a waste of money, but, what is sometimes worse, a waste of *impression*—for every time you wear these not-quite-right clothes, you create a false impression in the minds of all those who see you. How quickly you can acquire a reputation for carelessness, poor taste, and what not, by appearing, *even if only now and then* in these clothes that are just not quite right.

But you need no longer *ever* wear a single garment that is not just exactly up-to-the-minute in style and perfect in becomingness. No matter how limited your means, no matter how busy you are—you need never again wear anything but the m o s t fashionable and charming clothes, for the Institute tells you not only how to make stylish new garments, but also how to make over your

dresses, wraps, waists, and skirts of last year or previous seasons and give them this season's best style characteristics. Every detail of this work is covered—how to renovate materials and make them look fresh, how to recolor all kinds of goods, how to combine new and old materials to make a dress look entirely new, how to add a pretty touch here and there, how to alter collars, cuffs, or trimming, and how to wholly convert a garment and give it an entirely different appearance. With this knowledge you can keep your clothes always smart and pleasing, for you will know how to make those vitally important little alterations in the garments you have which will keep them always in step with fashion's changes.

Think what a saving this will mean to you. This knowledge alone will double the life of your clothes and give you twice the value for the money you spend. A member in Nebraska says: "I made an afternoon dress out of my graduation frock of five years ago. I dyed the white crêpe de Chine a pretty dark blue and made it up with frills and a panel and lengthened the waist. The only things purchased were 30 inches of belting and 1½ yards of satin ribbon and a package of dye, costing altogether $1.10, and the new frock is worth at least $25."

Lovely Make-Overs at Little Cost

I am preparing my 19-year-old daughter for college. She is so proud of her dresses and has so many more than usual. I have taken out-of-style dresses and made beautiful new ones. The only expense would be for trimming or something to combine with them. I copied a taffeta model, priced $24.50 for $2.85 and a tissue gingham marked $19.50, for $3.25. The Institute has brought a new happiness into our home. My husband is always complimenting me on the things I make.

MRS. E. A. SHERRILL,
Beaumont, Texas

Originally published in "How You Can Have More and Prettier Clothes" Book, 1925

You Will Learn to Make Practical Maternity Clothes

AT no other time in a woman's life is the ability to make clothes so important—or so precious—as when she is about to become a mother. Her own clothes, at this period, must be comfortable, and they must be cleverly designed to cover, gracefully, the changing curves of her figure.

It is always difficult to *buy* satisfactory maternity clothes. In some places, indeed, it is impossible to get them, and women have no other course but to buy ordinary styles, in large sizes. And these are invariably unsatisfactory—too large in the beginning and too clumsy later on. At best, they are makeshifts. And in places where it *is* possible to buy maternity clothes, they are too often very *obviously* such, and they are invariably high-priced.

So high, indeed, is the price of these clothes that the prospective mother usually buys only one, or, at most two, dresses for these months. And oh, how weary she gets of wearing those dresses!

There is only one sensible thing to do in the matter of maternity clothes, and that is to learn to make them yourself — especially when it is so easy to learn by the Institute's new method. After only a few lessons in this new course, you will be able to make maternity clothes that are correctly and cleverly designed for their purpose, and that are, at the same time, attractive, graceful, and even smart.

Best of all, you need not stint on your clothes at this time when, above all others, you should be surrounded by beauty and variety. You can make yourself as many lovely dresses, wraps, etc. at this time as at any other—first because you will be able to make clothes at such a trifling cost, and, second, because after the baby comes, you need not discard your maternity clothes, for you will easily learn to remodel them to fit you and to look like smart, new dresses!

And an Exquisite Layette for Baby

Of course, the sweetest thing the prospective mother has to do is to prepare a layette for the little one who is to come. Indeed, the woman who *buys* her baby's little dresses, coats, caps, petticoats, nightgowns, etc., is missing one of the most beautiful experiences that life has to offer.

The Woman's Institute offers expectant mothers a worthy service not only in giving detailed instructions for making by hand the daintiest, finest, and most appropriate garments for infants but in furnishing the mother with a complete list of all the little garments the baby will need.

Here is a service which the Woman's Institute is glad and proud to perform, and one which has brought comfort and inspiration to many hundreds of expectant mothers.

There is another special value in this instruction and that is that the making of layettes and infants' clothing is one of the most interesting and profitable ways to earn money at home.

In almost every city there are specialty shops catering to those who insist upon having only the finest of hand-made garments for baby's wardrobe. Such shops and also the department stores are glad to find women or girls who can do really exquisite work and to pay them well for all the sewing and embroidering they care to do at any time.

Many Institute students have splendid incomes from such work and many others have opened little specialty shops of their own. In fact, this is just another example of the instruction on one subject being worth the cost of the entire course.

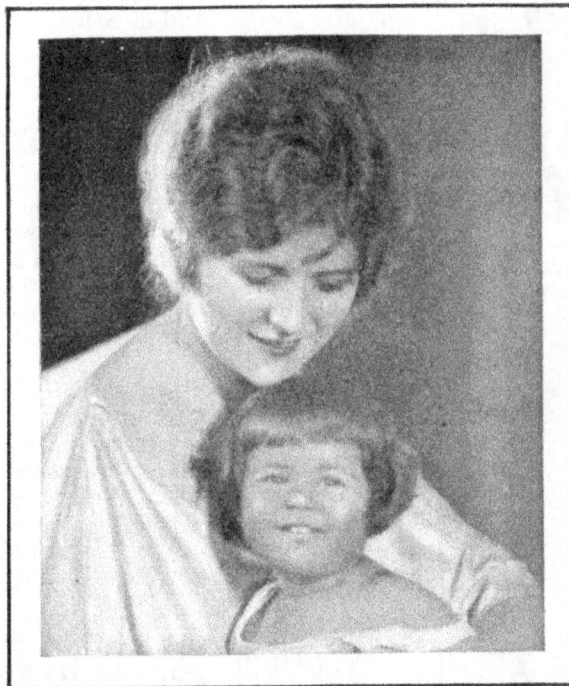

Finds Joy in Making Layette

"My little layette is progressing nicely. I can copy the most expensive imported things at a wee per cent. of their cost in the shops. For instance one little dress with handrun tucks, a tiny spray of embroidery and scalloped lower edge finished with lace was marked $25. I copied it in even nicer material for about $3. I know my little one will have as fine and dainty garments as the wealthiest child and besides the great saving I have had the joy of making them myself."

MRS. KATHLEEN BIRD, Miami, Okla.

Originally published in "How You Can Have More and Prettier Clothes" Book, 1925

You Can Now Have All the Lovely Underwear and Lingerie You Want

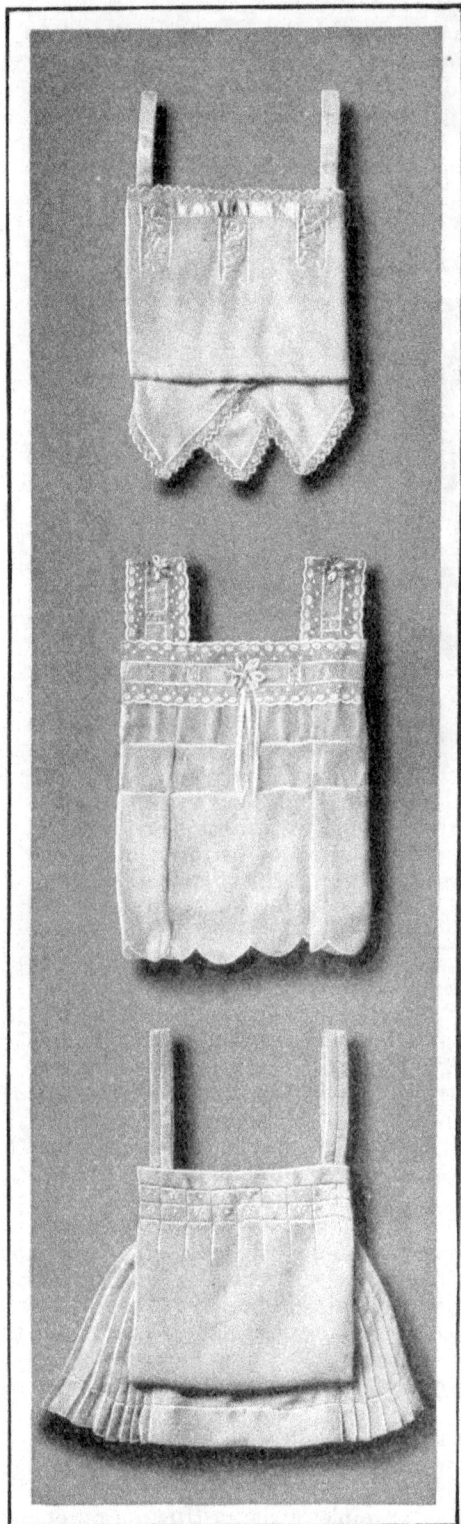

I F you are like most other women, the lovely silk and lacy underthings you see advertised or in the shops tempt you, sometimes, to extravagance—for what woman does not love to indulge occasionally, in really fine, dainty undergarments?

But, of course, they *are* an extravagance—unless you make them yourself. In that case, they are an economy, as well as a delight, for you can *easily* learn to make yourself the greatest variety of exquisite, excellent quality undergarments at far *less* than the price you ordinarily have to pay for them. And of course, the ones you make will not only look lovelier, wear better, and last longer, but they will *fit* you perfectly, as almost no ready-made undergarment does.

In fact, more and more women are coming to realize the importance of properly cut and finished undergarments. If they are cut on lines designed for your figure and made correctly, you can be sure your outer garments will fit better and you will have that sense of moving easily and gracefully in your clothes which gives comfort. Especially if you are inclined to be at all stout, you will be astonished at how much slenderer and neater you will look if your outer clothes hang smoothly over well-made, smooth-fitting underthings.

The Woman's Institute Course shows you simply and explicitly just how to cut, finish, and trim any kind of underwear from the so-called tailored styles to the more elaborately lace trimmed and embroidered garments. It explains just how to make them fit easily and well and how to "stay" them at important places for wear. This instruction comes early in your course so that you may have properly fitting underwear when you begin making your own dresses, coats, and suits.

You Will Learn to Do All Kinds of Hand Embroidery and Fancy Work

Hand embroidery is to a gown, wrap, undergarment, or child's frock what frosting is to a cake. It can be the touch of artistry that makes all the difference between an ordinary *type* of dress and an exclusive model of individuality and dainty distinction.

The note of color, the dash of smartness, the touch of originality and refinement which hand work gives to a garment—all these are effects well worth achieving—and you *can* achieve them so easily and so delightfully by the Woman's Institute method of teaching.

Whether it be embroidery, hemstitching, drawn work, beading, braiding, or any other kind of hand work you may want to put on a garment, you can learn *exactly* how to do it in the simplest way.

Do you realize that there are 108 decorative embroidery stitches? In this course every stitch is described minutely, and the process of making it is beautifully and clearly pictured. You learn the kinds of needles and floss required for the various stitches and the best materials to use. In fact, this instruction is virtually a complete course in itself.

Originally published in "How You Can Have More and Prettier Clothes" Book, 1925

You Can Make the Loveliest Linens, Curtains, Draperies and Pillows

DO not think that through the Institute Course you learn only to make clothes. No, indeed. You learn not only to make every type of garment, but to do every other kind of sewing and needlework as well. In fact, the Course is so complete that no matter what you may want to make for yourself or for your home, if it can be made with needle and thread and materials, you will know just how to create it with your own hands at a mere fraction of the cost to buy it.

Have you any idea how much money you spend unnecessarily every year on household accessories? Your curtains, bureau scarfs, table runners, table cloths, napkins, towels, sheets, pillow cases, even your heavy draperies and hangings, all these can be beautifully made at home at a substantial saving.

You Can Have Pretty New Curtains for Every Room

Think what a delight it will be to be able to beautify your home with lovely hangings—gay chintzes or dimity for summer—heavy silks or velvets, for winter. And your curtains! You will no longer have to keep on making your old curtains do, year after year. Now, in a very short time, and at the most trifling expenditure, you can learn to make all kinds of new curtains, whenever you want them—dainty, frilled, dotted swiss or point d'esprit ones for the bedroom, pretty ones of scrim or voile for the children's room, with perhaps some charming little designs embroidered in colored worsted or appliquéd on with bits of colored cotton scraps. You will even be able to make exquisite casement curtains or French door curtains, for living or dining room—the kind that you have often admired in the homes of your friends and yet are so expensive when you purchase them outright.

Now You Can Afford Lovely Linens

And of course you can make all your own bed coverings and table linens. Formerly expensive materials were thought necessary, but now the preference is for those beautifully made and finished, those that show good taste and harmonize perfectly in color and design with their surroundings. By hemstitching or embroidering them yourself, you can, without paying a cent for anything but the material, make for yourself the handsomest household linens that can be procured anywhere.

And if you wish to make money on your work, this is one of the most profitable ways of doing it. There is always a demand for beautifully monogrammed, scalloped, hand-hemstitched, lace-edged or otherwise hand-decorated household linens, and the hand work on these makes them very valuable and they always command the very highest prices. Indeed, this kind of hand work is the most profitable kind of needlework, for, without any expenditure on your part at all, except for needles and thread, it increases the value of the material three, five, and often tenfold.

Originally published in "How You Can Have More and Prettier Clothes" Book, 1925

Your Little Ones Can Be the Best Dressed Children in the Neighborhood

NOTHING quite so delights a mother's heart as to be able to dress her children attractively. Every mother longs to have for her children the many clothes needed to keep little folks fresh and dainty. She knows, too, how rapidly the little ones outgrow dresses, coats, and underwear, although the material in them is still good. The Woman's Institute Course will teach you how to make the prettiest and most stylish little garments for your children at less than half what they would cost you ready made. It will also show you how to utilize the old or outgrown clothes of the family by making them over for the children in a great variety of clever and becoming ways.

Thousands of mothers write us that the Institute's greatest service to them has been the solving of this problem of their children's clothes. If you have children, you will find this one of the first and most delightful benefits of your course. For we teach you how to make every garment you may need or that your heart may desire for children of all ages.

You can learn how to plan and make dresses and rompers for the toddlers, or shirts and pants and suits and coats for sturdy boys.

If you have a daughter, you can plan and make dresses suited to her own particular type, to bring out her particular charm, to make her pretty and graceful and well appearing wherever she may go. And every mother knows what an important bearing pretty, becoming clothes have in the development of character, poise, and confidence in the growing girl. No matter whether she is a little girl just off to school, or in that period from twelve to sixteen when you find it so hard to dress her becomingly, or

when she is first realizing the charm of delightfully becoming clothes—no matter what her age or size—the Woman's Institute Course will teach you just how to dress her correctly, in the way that makes her most attractive.

Joy in this Mother's Heart

A member in Utah says: "I made my four girls each two nice gingham dresses and saved enough to buy voile for a nice white dress for each of them. For my little boy I made three nice wash suits and saved enough to buy navy blue serge for his winter suit. And all these little garments are finished so neatly and done so quickly that they are a joy to my heart. What is more I have stopped worrying about what would become of the children if we were left alone."

Do not imagine that you will learn to make only women's garments. The Woman's Institute course is designed to be a *real* help to the home woman, and it teaches you, therefore, to make many kinds of garments for the men in the family as well as for the women.

Not only will you learn how to cut down your husband's old suits, shirts, etc. into attractive little tailored suits, rompers, shirts, etc. for your little boys —but you will learn to make all sorts of tailored garments for your big boys as well. Not only shirts and pajamas, but bathrobes, house coats, knickers, and even tailored suits and overcoats for boys are among the things you can learn to make.

One mother writes: "I have made nine little shirts for my boys from shirts my husband had worn. He says my course is the best investment we ever made."

Hers the "Best Dressed Children in Town"

I am sewing for myself now and the two children. My little girl who is four, has never had a piece of ready made clothing and she has the reputation of being the best-dressed child in town. The boy is just passing out of the romper class into real pants, and I feel that I am just as capable of putting in pockets for him as I am of making dainty things for the girl. You can see from this how much the Woman's Institute has meant to me. Just to hear my daughter referred to as the "best-dressed child in town" is in itself worth every cent I paid for my Course.

MRS. JOHN E. WISE, Onancock, Virginia.

Originally published in "How You Can Have More and Prettier Clothes" Book, 1925

Vintage Notions Monthly continues to share the work of Mary Brooks Picken and the Woman's Institute which inspired my book *Vintage Notions*. Although the Institute was founded 100 years ago, the treasure trove of lessons and stories are still relevant today and offer a blueprint for living a contented life.

If you enjoyed this issue of *Vintage Notions Monthly*, visit AmyBarickman.com for more of my curated collection of vintage content including patterns and books for needle and thread, inspiring fabric, textiles & free vintage art. Be sure to subscribe to my **Amy Barickman Studio YouTube Channel** where I share fascinating sewing and fashion history along with timeless style and DIY technique for your modern making!

www.amybarickman.com
Subscribe to my eNewsletters
Follow my creative journey!
Learn about new products, videos, special offers, and receive a FREE PDF gift filled with *Vintage Made Modern* printable and a Cropped Jacket Magic Pattern.

Join my Community
Further your skills and enhance your knowledge with fellow vintage-inspired creative spirits!
Amy Barickman's Vintage Made Modern Facebook Group
Amy Barickman Studio YouTube Channel
Amy Barickman Studio Facebook Page
AmyBarickman Studio Instagram

Inspiration Vintage Notions Monthly, Volume 1, Issue 3 (VN0103)

All rights reserved. Printed in USA. No part of this publication covered by the copyrights herein may be used in any form of reproduced by any means—graphic, electronic, or mechanical, including photocopying, recording, except for excerpts in the context for reviews, without written permission of the publisher. Purchasing this book represents agreement that the buyer will use this book for personal use only, not for reproduction or resale in whole or in part. The original, rare content is in the public domain;however this restored and revised edition has been created from my personal collection and is protected by copyright.

To reach Amy email amyb@amybarickman.com

www.ingramcontent.com/pod-product-compliance
Lightning Source LLC
LaVergne TN
LVHW061330060426
835513LV00015B/1353